GOING
FOR THE
GOLD

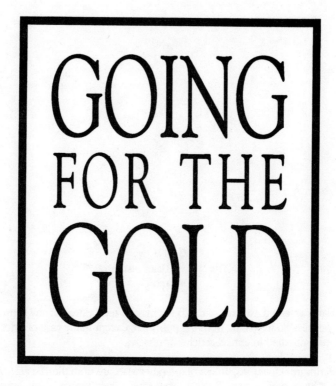

GOING
FOR THE
GOLD

JOE L. WALL

MOODY PRESS
CHICAGO

1 2 3 4 5 6 Printing/BC/Year 95 94 93 92 91

Printed in the United States of America

Contents

Therefore we make it our aim, whether present or absent, to be well pleasing to Him. For we must all appear before the judgment seat of Christ, that each one may receive the things done in the body, according to what he has done, whether good or bad.

2 Corinthians 5:9-10

But why do you judge your brother? Or why do you show contempt for your brother? For we shall all stand before the judgment seat of Christ.

Romans 14:10

Acknowledgments

I would like to express my appreciation to a number of people who have made this book possible through their encouragement and input. My wife, Linda, and sons, Scot and Christopher, were a continual encouragement to complete the project. Our good friends Don and Gwynne Johnson were also of great encouragement. The critique and input of an earlier draft by Charles Ryrie, Zane Hodges, Dwight Pentecost, and two colleagues at the university, Frank Ames and Liam Atchison, contributed greatly to the finished product.

Foreword

The downhill slalom racer was greeted at the bottom of the course by his ski coach: "The good news is that you arrived at the finish marker faster than any of my other students. In fact, your time was the fastest ever on this course, perhaps even faster than the world record!

"The bad news is that when you miss even one flag, you are disqualified." To which the novice slalom skier replied, "Flags? What flags?"

A good slalom racer understands that the route taken to get downhill is more important than just reaching the goal. Any basketball player understands that making a basket is not as important as making sure he is aiming toward the *right* basket. In most sports, both the goal and the manner of attaining the goal are vital.

Yet what is often remembered in sports is too often forgotten in the Christian walk. We have lost sight of which of our acts will be rewarded in heaven and which will be disqualified as missing the flags of proper motivations, godly direction, and willful obedience. We have lost a sense of heaven and therefore have lost a sense of how this life is to be lived for eternal impact.

Standing at the starting gate, halfway down the hill, coming in toward the final stretch, we all have similar questions:

1. Will a Christian really have to give an account for his life?
2. What really happens when I die?
3. Isn't it wrong to have a motive to gain eternal rewards?

By describing what Scripture has to say about the awards banquet of heaven, Joe Wall provides us with a guide for finding our direction again. Reading about this crucial event in a believer's experience leaves no doubt that what we do now greatly affects what we'll do in eternity. We gain a clear picture of what heaven is like and what we must do on earth to make our lives count.

I've known Joe for more than thirty years. I've followed him through his career as a seminary student, then as a pastor in rural, suburban, and urban churches. I've enjoyed his Bible scholarship as he served as an academic dean at Dallas Bible College, co-founded the Houston Bible Institute, and now serves as president of Colorado Christian University. I've enjoyed him as a teacher as we've spoken at conferences and as he's sat in my office many times sharing the fascinating insights of a man of God so widely experienced.

Joe is a man committed to accurately interpreting God's Word, to compassionately ministering to those in his care, and to single-mindedly focusing on the end goal of what God has determined makes a life successful. It is no surprise to me that Joe would finally write on the topic of eternal rewards, since this is a perspective he not only teaches but lives.

HOWARD G. HENDRICKS

Preface

Some years ago, when I was pastoring a church in Houston, Texas, I delivered a preaching series on the subject of heavenly rewards and the judgment seat of Christ. My original plan had been to preach a short series of three or four messages. But as I prepared my messages, my plans began to change. I was confronted in a new way with many passages that shed light on the subject of rewards and was struck anew by how many references and allusions there are in the New Testament to rewards and the judgment seat of Christ. My four-week series expanded to five months.

Since that time I have taught on the subject of the judgment seat of Christ many times in conferences and on the radio. More recently at the historic Church of the Open Door in California, I preached a nine-part series on this crucial subject. It is primarily that series that is the basis for this book.

My interest in the biblical teaching on the judgment seat of Christ is more than academic. This doctrine has had a profound impact on my life in a number of ways. It has become a framework for making decisions. It has served—and continues to serve—as a purifying truth in my life. And it is a continual basis for encouragement in the face of unfair criticism.

My interest in the judgment seat of Christ goes back to my early days as a Christian. After becoming a Christian as a young teenager, I attended a Bible study taught by a man devoted to in-depth doctrinal teaching. Under his instruction I first heard what the Bible had to say about the judgment seat of Christ and began to understand that every thought, every word, every deed, and every motive will one day be evaluated by Jesus. So while still in high school, I began making life decisions based on an awareness that someday I would have to give account of my life to Jesus.

Over time, this truth touched every area of my life—where I should go to school, what I should study, what I should seek to accomplish in life. I found myself sorting through my habits, my decisions, my activities, trying to see myself and my life just as Christ might when I stand before Him on that great day.

As I studied the Bible further, I became convinced that the reality of Christ's judgment seat is an essential doctrine that can and should inspire godly living. Jesus can return at any moment. What we do and think in private will then be made public.

Not only did this great doctrine affect my decision making and my daily walk, it also provided great encouragement on numerous occasions. I came to see that Christ will not only judge my shortcomings, He will also vindicate me where others have wrongly accused or convicted me. If no one else comprehends what I am doing or what motivates me, Jesus does—and one day He will make known the truth about my life, both reproving me and rewarding me accordingly.

When one accepts leadership responsibilities in the ministry, as in any business or profession, criticism and unfair accusations come with the territory. Even in hard times, when difficult decisions have to be made, there are still those who are quick to judge your wisdom and even your motives. During those times, one major biblical truth can provide reassurance and encouragement: the biblical teaching that Jesus Christ will someday set the record straight at His judgment seat.

The Judgment and Rewards series, upon which this book is based, has always generated curiosity and questions, and sometimes even debate. But most important, through a systematic discussion of this great truth, nur..erous men and women —perhaps for the very first time—begin to grasp the eternal significance of the way they live.

It is my desire that this study will cause you, the reader, to be more sober and alert to the eternal importance of your decisions, words, thoughts, and actions. And I pray, too, that it will arouse within you a profound love for the appearing of our Lord and Savior, Jesus Christ.

JOE L. WALL
President, Colorado Christian University

Part 1

THE JUDGMENT SEAT OF CHRIST

1

In the Presence of the King

The scene is breathtaking. You have died, and the Lord has come for those who believe in Him. You have been joined to your resurrection body and now stand in the presence of your glorious Savior, the matchless Lord of the church, the absolute Monarch of the entire creation.

Your life flashes before you with three-dimensional vividness and stereophonic clarity (1 Corinthians 3:13). Your beloved Lord publicly sets the record straight. All the false accusations, lies, and unfair criticisms you received in life are exposed for what they really were—full vindication at last (Romans 14:6-12; 1 Corinthians 4:3,5; 2 Thessalonians 1:4-10)! Jesus then examines all that you have said, thought, and done in the light of your purposes and motives. Why did you do that? Why didn't you do this? (Romans 14:12). His fiery eye reveals the true value of all that you have brought before Him (Revelation 1:14; 1 Corinthians 3:13).

You are awestruck and defenseless as you hear Jesus' declaration of all that is worthless and sinful, and you are pierced with a deep sense of shame (1 John 2:28). Your true spiritual maturity in life is examined, and He decrees the kind of welcome you will experience when you enter His glorious kingdom (2 Peter 1:11).

You are commended publicly for your faithful service (Matthew 25:21) and for your public loyalty to Him (Luke 12:8, 9). Then He awards you incorruptible symbols of honor that are accompanied with the announcement of your responsibilities in Jesus' glorious eternal kingdom. Because Jesus Himself is ultimately the source of all that is good in your life, He is glorified by every honor He bestows on you.

You have just been through the judgment seat (*bema*) of Christ.[1]

JUDGMENT BEFORE THE *BEMA*

Judgment at the *bema?*

Yes, the *bema*, the Greek term for the place of evaluation before Christ that believers will face after the return of Christ for His own and they are caught up in the air to be with Him forever. The *bema* judgment takes place in heaven and is an evaluation of the believer's life, not a judgment as to salvation. It is a moment when every believer will give an account of his life to the Lord—when every word, every deed, every thought, and every motive will be revealed and judged by the Lord Jesus Christ.

Recently a Bible teacher at a Christian high school asked his students to write out what they would say to the Lord if they suddenly died and came face-to-face with Him. Though all the students worded it differently, nearly every one said something like this: "Lord, I know I have not really been living like I should as a Christian. In fact, I've been doing some terrible things that the Bible teaches I shouldn't do. But because I trusted You as my Savior when I was seven years old, You won't judge me for those things; everything is wonderful now that I am with You and will be with You forever."

Intuitively we know there is something missing in an answer like that. Yet many adult Christians would answer in a similar way. Even without the words, far too many Christians today, particularly in North America, say by their actions if not by their words, "Lord, I know I'm not living for You. But because I have made a salvation decision, one day I will be with You and You won't hold me responsible for anything else."

Does the Lord—or *will* the Lord—hold us responsible for what we do in this life once we have received Him as Savior? Either the answer to this question is no, meaning there is no reason to live according to God's will unless it is for personal benefits in the here and now, or the answer is a resounding yes, meaning that God has established an accountability system, a basis of future evaluation, intended solely for believers.

In this book we are going to see that the answer indeed is a resounding yes. The Lord does and will hold us accountable for what we do in this life, and that evaluation will occur at the *bema*. If that is true, why has so little been said about this evaluation? The primary reason believers of our generation have failed to affirm this biblical fact is that they have confused the evaluation of Christians with the judgment of non-Christians, or, to put it another way, they have confused *stewardship* with *salvation*. For unbelievers, the issue is salvation. Trust Jesus Christ as Savior in this life, or be judged in God's presence after this life. For believers, however, the issue is quite different. For them, it has to do with stewardship, accountability, and responsibility. Serve Jesus Christ in this life, for in a coming day you will have to stand before Christ and give a full accounting of your life on earth.

This book, then, is about that judgment and the eternal rewards to follow. It focuses on the great event that one day will take place in heaven, the "judgment seat of Christ," or as the Greek New Testament calls it, the "*bema* of Christ."

A DOCTRINE THAT CAN CHANGE YOUR LIFE

The Bible describes the judgment seat of Christ for one main purpose: to affect the way we think and live—to motivate us to anticipate with joy His return and to live our lives to please Him, not worrying about the way others treat us or what they may think about us.

Some time ago when I was pastoring a church in Texas, I especially looked forward to Mondays. Monday was the day I could "let it all hang out." My fellow pastor, Ronnie, and I frequently used our Monday golf game as a way to dispel our Sunday frustrations.

One day as I teed up my ball, I muttered,"You know, Ronnie, sometimes I really get frustrated with some church people. I put in fifty to sixty hours a week, and all it ever earns me is more griping and criticism."

Just as I pulled back my club to swing, my wise friend chirped, "But you know, Joe, it'll all come out at the *bema,* so don't worry about it."

He was exactly right!

Ultimately, everything will come out at the *bema,* where Jesus' point of view will be evident—and after all, His point of view is the only one that really matters! Furthermore, Jesus will make sure that those who should know about us will see us with His perception. If we need vindication, we will have it. If we deserve commendation, we will receive it. If our motives, our thoughts, or our deeds require rebuke, we will suffer under His disappointed gaze. All will be laid bare, and all will be lovingly and perfectly examined by the Master.

Recognizing the importance of this doctrine, Wilbur Smith had this to say about it in an article in *Eternity* magazine:

> [The] whole subject of rewards for the believer is one, I am afraid, rarely thought of by the ordinary Christian, or even the average student of the Scriptures. But it is both a joyous and solemn theme and should serve as a potent incentive for holiness of life.[2]

A Positive Motivation to Holy Living

One of the great burdens expressed by many ministers is the chasm that too often exists between the lifestyle the Christian church teaches and the lifestyle lived out by church members and leaders. Reacting to this hypocrisy, some have attempted to press their people into godly living through preaching the danger of hell. Some preach that one is not truly saved through simple trust in Christ and His wonderful saving work through the cross and His resurrection, but that one must have a deep, committed, persevering faith before he can ever begin to have any true assurance of his salvation. It is a shame that such an approach should be entertained, for it comes dangerously close to preaching a gospel different from the gospel of grace taught in Scripture (Galatians 1:6-9; 3:1-5; 2 Corinthians 11:4).

Certainly the terrible moral compromise and wide ranging lack of commitment by God's people should alarm us. However, the answer to this kind of problem in the church should not be that we push the gospel of grace toward works-salvation. Rather the Scriptures provide three other strong motivations for holy living without diluting the concept of salvation by grace.

First, the Bible repeatedly teaches that the true Christian has been regenerated (John 3:1-16) and indwelt by the Holy Spirit (1 Corinthians 6:19). Thus all true believers are new people on the inside, and the living God lives on the inside of them. Because we have been forgiven and given life for free, based on the loving sacrifice of Christ, in response to His love we commit to His lordship in our lives (Romans 12:1, 2).

Second, because God is our Father, He promises to discipline us if we continue to rebel against His direction and correction, and we are thus motivated by a fear of fatherly discipline (Hebrews 12:3-17).

Third, and finally, the fact that we will one day have to give account of our lives to Jesus before His judgment seat is a sobering truth that should affect the way we live.

Though not the only motivating factor, I am convinced that the doctrine of the judgment seat (*bema*) is meant to be one of the major scriptural motivations for godly living. The Scriptures bear this out by relating rewards and the *bema* to a number of "Christian living" truths.

AN INCENTIVE TO GODLY PRIORITIES AND WISE DECISION MAKING

Believing the biblical teaching about rewards should significantly affect our priorities and decision making.

1. If we keep our eyes on the end of the race and our appearing in the presence of the Lord Jesus, we will set proper goals for our lives (Philippians 3:8-14).

2. If we truly understand the doctrine of rewards, we will maintain an appropriate attitude toward the stewardship of our wealth, time, and energy (Matthew 6:1-4, 19-21).

3. If we fulfill God's plan for our lives, lovingly anticipating Christ's return, we will be greatly rewarded (2 Timothy 4:6-8).

4. If we minister to others through evangelism and discipleship, we may receive one of the highest eternal rewards (1 Thessalonians 2:1-20).

5. For those considering places of leadership in the church, knowledge that Jesus has prepared a special crown for faithful leadership will be a strong motive to take on such weighty responsibilities.

A MOTIVATION TO A DEEPER SPIRITUAL LIFE

A serious consideration of giving account of our lives to Jesus at the *bema* will produce a deeper—and more practical —spiritual life.

1. The Christian who is eagerly looking for the return of Christ will be motivated to be pure in his walk (1 John 2:28-3:3).

2. A *bema* perspective will remind us to confess our sins—keeping short accounts with God (1 John 1:9; 2:28).

3. Looking forward to our entrance into the messianic kingdom will alert us to the importance of maturing spiritually (2 Peter 1:5-11).

4. As we look forward to eternal rewards and the promise of our inheritance, we will be encouraged in our walk of faith (Hebrews 11:6, 39-40; 12:17).

5. A persevering faith in the face of suffering will earn great reward (James 1:12; Revelation 2:10).

6. A realistic view of the judgment seat of Christ will give a desire to walk in the Spirit (Galatians 5:16-6:9).

A SOURCE OF ENCOURAGEMENT AND COMFORT

Much that is written about our appearance before the Lord is provided for our encouragement and comfort.

1. In the face of bereavement or persecution, we can receive comfort through the hope of Jesus' return and the promise of His vindication (John 14:1-3; 2 Thessalonians 1:4-10).
2. In the face of criticism, the truth that Jesus ultimately will reveal all the facts and declare His evaluation of us can be a tremendous encouragement (Romans 14:1-13).

This book will address these and other crucial subjects related to the Christian life in the context of one of the most profound and motivating studies in the New Testament—the doctrine of rewards and the *bema* of Jesus Christ.

Notes

1. This scenario of the way the *bema* will be carried out is an attempt to pull together the teachings on the subject from a number of passages. The precise order is not summarily presented in Scripture; however, all of the elements indeed will be there.
2. Wilbur Smith, "Inheritance and Reward in Heaven," *Eternity*, March 1977, p. 79.

2

The Judgments of Christ

Over the years I have learned that what the Bible teaches concerning the judgment seat of Christ can arouse strong reactions, even protests, from believers.

"A special judgment for Christians? But I thought all of us were freely forgiven by God, because Jesus died for us. Doesn't the Bible teach that no one who is in Christ Jesus will ever be condemned?"

Absolutely correct!

"And doesn't the Bible teach that we are saved from judgment by grace, without good works?"

Right!

"Isn't Jesus' judgment that condemns people to hell reserved only for those who have never accepted His free gift of forgiveness?"

Right again!

"Then how in the world can a Christian's works ever be judged?"

The answer to that question lies in an understanding of what the Bible teaches on the subject of judgment in God's overall prophetic plan. The Bible speaks of judgment in two distinct doctrinal categories. Category one has to do with divine judgment of unbelievers, that is, of those persons who have never trusted Jesus Christ for divine forgiveness. Category two has to do with judgment of believers. The following pages contain a summary of the biblical teachings on judgment. More details of the major prophetic events as they relate to coming judgment are found in chapter 6.

JUDGMENT OF UNBELIEVERS

According to the Bible, God's judgment will focus on unbelievers during three different periods. The Bible also teaches that the Father gave to Jesus—the Messiah—full authority to carry out or execute all of these judgments (John 5:22-29).

JUDGMENT IN THE TRIBULATION PERIOD

First, the Bible prophesies that there will be a seven-year period of judgment called the Tribulation period (Daniel 9:27; Matthew 24:15-21). During the last, terrifying three and a half years of this time, Jesus Christ will express the holy indignation of God as He pours out unquenchable wrath upon the world. This is described in detail in the book of Revelation (chapters 5-18).

JUDGMENT AT THE SECOND ADVENT

When Jesus returns to the earth in triumph at the end of the Tribulation period, He will judge the nations. Commonly known as the second advent, this second coming climaxes this evil age and introduces the messianic age of peace and righteousness.

Israel and the Gentile nations will be judged, and those who are believers will be ushered into the messianic kingdom. Those who are not believers, will be cast into the "everlasting fire prepared for the devil and his angels." (See Matthew 24-25.)

JUDGMENT AT THE GREAT WHITE THRONE

The last judgment of unbelievers will take place before the great white throne and is often called the great white throne judgment. At the end of the first phase of the messianic kingdom (which we call the Millennium because it will be one thousand years in length) Jesus will judge everyone who has rejected God's provision of salvation by grace.

The biblical picture of the great white throne room is straightforward and to the point. Jesus sits on His throne (John 5), and everybody who does not know Christ as Savior stands before Him to be judged (Revelation 20).

Let's listen in.

Sam Didhisbest is standing in the presence of King Jesus. Jesus has two sets of books as a resource for His judgment. Set number one is a collection of books registering everything Sam ever did in life, good or bad. The second set has only one large book called the Book of Life.

First the Lord evaluates everything Sam has ever done—all the good things and all the bad things. There is one major problem, however. Isaiah, the Hebrew prophet, states that all of our righteous deeds are as filthy rags in the presence of a perfect, holy God (Isaiah 64:6). And Paul in the New Testament echoes that truth: "There is none righteous, no not one" (Romans 3:10). "All have sinned and come short of the glory of God" (Romans 3:23).

"Sam, your life doesn't meet God's high, holy standards. You stand condemned by God. Hell is your destiny, that is, unless your name is written in this other book, the Lamb's Book of Life."

A brief silence is followed by the cold truth. "Sam, the record is clear. You're not in this book. That means you felt you didn't need Me or anything I had to offer when I came as a sacrificial lamb to pay the penalty for your sins. You wanted to go it on your own. You wanted to earn whatever you get from Me. So be it. The Scriptures state that the wages of sin is spiritual death."

Not only Sam Didhisbest but everyone who stands at the great white throne judgment, we are told, will be cast into the lake of fire—the final judgment awaiting those whose names are not written in the Lamb's Book of Life (Revelation 20:15).

THE JUDGMENT OF BELIEVERS

Now the good news. Everyone who has trusted in Christ has his name written in the Lamb's Book of Life and thus has been saved from the awful judgment of the great white throne (Revelation 7:14; 20:11-15; 1 Thessalonians 1:10). "There is therefore now no condemnation to those who are in Christ Jesus" (Romans 8:1*a*).

There are only two kinds of judgment for the believer. God judges the believer at the cross and at the *bema*. Two times we are judged. We go through no other judgments if we are believers in Jesus Christ.

JUDGMENT AT THE CROSS

The first judgment of the believer is the judgment at the cross. Because God loved us with an infinite love, God the Father poured out judgment on Jesus on the cross. That was *our* judgment also. Jesus was judged in our place: He paid the penalty for our sins so that we would not have to pay for them in the lake of fire (John 3:16, 36).

The primary reason Jesus Christ came into the world was to die and conquer death. When He died, He hung on the cross from 9:00 A.M. until 3:00 P.M. A great darkness covered the land for the last three hours. During that terrible time Jesus cried out, "Eloi, Eloi, lama sabachthani," Aramaic for "My God, My God, why have You forsaken Me!" (Mark 15:34)[1], indicating that He was suffering the pain of separation from His father in heaven. At that time Jesus Christ "became sin for us that we might become the righteousness of God in Him" (2 Corinthians 5:21).

While Christ hung upon the cross, the Father was saying in effect, "You are suffering hell for everyone who has ever lived —and for everyone who is ever going to live" (see Romans 5:8). So Jesus Christ died on the cross, and in so doing took our place. In effect, we were judged then also.

A number of years ago, late one Sunday night, I was driving into Houston traveling about 55 MPH. I failed to see a speed limit sign that read 35 MPH. No problem. No one was on the road but me. No one could get hurt. No policemen around—I thought. But I was wrong. Two police cars were driving in the parking lot of a nearby shopping center. They stopped me and gave me a ticket.

Some two weeks later, I went to court. The arresting officer was there also. As the judge dispatched each case, I thought about what I should say. I noticed that a number of the people were pleading "guilty with explanation," which sounded good to me. When my turn came, I stood before the judge and said, "Judge, I plead guilty with explanation. I was sleepy, no one else was on the road, and I didn't see the speed limit sign."

The judge turned to the officer, "Was this preacher impolite to you?"

"No, he was too sleepy."

"Do you think that if I give this young preacher a five dollar fine it will slow him down?"

"Sure," the officer replied. So I paid my five dollars, got my receipt, and left.

Suppose I had said to the judge, "I'm sorry, but I don't have five dollars." Now at that point he had already ruled me guilty, so he would have been justified in responding, "That's not my problem. Pay the state five dollars or spend five days in jail."

I would have been on my way to jail for five days!

But let's suppose that the back door of the courtroom opened and my father came running in, waving a five-dollar bill. Suppose he dashed up to the judge, slapped the bill down on the judge's desk, and said, "Judge, I'll pay the penalty. Take the five dollars, or take me. I love this boy and I will pay whatever debt he owes." All I would have to do would be to say, "I believe in my father, and I'll let him pay the penalty for me." I would leave with no charge against me.

That is similar to what Jesus did for all of us. All we have to do is accept for free what Jesus did for us. He comes into the presence of the Father and says, "Father, I don't want Joe to have to go through the great white throne judgment. I have already taken his hell for him."

I trust Jesus, and God counts Jesus' completed judgment as mine. I stand totally free from condemnation forever.

One might ask, "How could one man pay the penalty of eternal condemnation for so many sins by so many people in just a few hours on the cross?"

He could do so for two reasons. Jesus was infinitely valuable and could take the place of an infinite number of people. And because He was infinitely righteous, He could pay the penalty for an infinite number of sins.

Jesus Christ satisfied the justice of God, and therefore I was judged on the cross with Him. The moment I trusted in Christ as my Savior, I was also judged. I have had *my* hell. I have already paid the penalty through Jesus. There is no double jeopardy for the sin in my life. He paid the penalty for all my sins—past, present, and future. All were taken care of before the law court of God. "For He made Him who knew no sin to be sin for us, that we might become the righteousness of God in Him" (2 Corinthians 5:21).

We are "just" before God because of Jesus.

Charles Wesley captured this glorious truth in his classic hymn "And Can It Be That I Should Gain":

> And can it be that I should gain
> An int'rest in the Savior's blood?
> Died He for me, who caused His pain?
> For me, who Him to death pursued?
> Amazing love! how can it be
> That Thou, my God, shouldst die for me?
>
> No condemnation now I dread;
> Jesus, and all in Him, is mine!
> Alive in Him, my living Head,
> And clothed in righteousness divine,
> Bold I approach th'eternal throne,
> And claim the crown, through Christ my own.

JUDGMENT AT THE *BEMA*

Because of Christ's perfect payment for sin at the cross, the only other judgment facing the Christian is the judgment seat of Christ, or the *bema.* The issue of our eternal salvation has already been settled. There is now no condemnation for those who are in Christ Jesus. Our entrance into His eternal kingdom is secure, without a doubt! But as we shall see in the pages ahead, the Lord has not lost interest in what we do with the great salvation He has so freely provided. He is intimately concerned with how we live out our lives from the point of salvation by grace through faith.

Note

1. This is a quotation from Psalm 22:1, a messianic psalm that portrays the death of Christ prophetically. The psalm is written in Hebrew. Jesus gave the contemporary rendition of the passage, that is, in Aramaic, the commonly spoken language of that part of the world.

3

Judgment at the *Bema*

As we have seen in the previous chapter, those who have placed their personal faith in Jesus Christ have passed from spiritual death to eternal life. They have been irrevocably saved forever, and according to Christ Himself, nothing (not even their own will or power) can pluck them out of the Father's hand. They will never stand before the great white throne in heaven to be judged by their works in regard to salvation. There is no condemnation for those who are in Christ Jesus, because they have already been judged at the cross, where Jesus Himself paid the penalty levied against every person in the human race.

But as we have already mentioned, there is a second judgment for believers, one that is not related to eternal salvation. That is the judgment seat—or *bema*—of Christ, described by Paul in both 2 Corinthians and Romans:

> Therefore we make it our aim, whether present or absent, to be well pleasing to Him. For we must all appear before the judgment seat [*bema*] of Christ, that each one may receive the things done in the body, according to what he has done, whether good or bad. (2 Corinthians 5:9-10)

But why do you judge your brother? Or why do you show contempt for your brother? For we shall all stand before the judgment seat [*bema*] of Christ. (Romans 14:10)

The *bema* judgment is not a legal judgment. Sin and its consequences are not the issue. The cross canceled that penalty forever.

Instead, the *bema* is a time for family evaluation after this life, a time when Jesus evaluates our lives and our faithfulness to Him, not for condemnation but as a basis for rewards, rewards for the works we have done in the power of the Spirit of God.

THE MEANING OF THE TERM *BEMA*

If we understand the meaning of the Greek word *bema,* the term translated "judgment seat" in 2 Corinthians 5 and Romans 14, we can better comprehend the character of this judgment.

The word *bema* means platform, raised place, or step.[1] The term "was used to denote a raised place or platform, reached by steps, originally that at Athens in the Pnyx Hill, where was the place of assembly; from the platform orations were made."[2]

In the Greco-Roman world the Greek term was translated by the Latin word *tribunal.* The Roman term, *tribunal,* and the Greek term, *bema,* both referred to the platform upon which a ruler or judge placed his chair when he issued decrees or judgments.[3] It is used in this way in Matthew 27:19; John 19:13; and Acts 12:21; 18:12-17; 25:6, 10, 17.

The term also applied to the *bemas,* or *tribunals,* the Caesars and their generals carried into battle. At the end of a battle Caesar or a general sat on the tribunal to award crowns made of woven branches to those who had made heroic contributions to the winning of the battle.[4]

The term *bema* was used as well to refer to the platform in the Jewish synagogues from which the Scriptures were read aloud. There the rabbis pronounced the law, or judgments, of God.

Finally, the term *bema* was used for the place of judgment and the awarding of rewards at the Greek athletic competition in the Panhellenic festivals, such as the Isthmian and Olympic games. It is this last use of the term that Paul appears to have had in mind when he wrote about the *bema.*

THE *BEMA* AT THE OLYMPIC GAMES

At the Olympic Games the competitors reported the first day at daybreak. They each took an oath affirming that they were of pure Hellenic blood, had never committed a wrong, had trained faithfully, and would not resort to any underhandedness in competition.

Contests included footraces, wrestling, boxing, the pentathlon, horse races, and chariot races. At the end of the Olympic festival, contestants appeared before the platform of judgment, the *bema.* If the judge proclaimed that an individual had won and had not been disqualified for some reason, that competitor received a crown of olive branches.

As the victor, he would normally return to his home city for a hero's welcome. The townspeople, seeking to distinguish him, often would erect a statue in his honor, give him choice seats at public events, and exempt him from taxes.[5]

PAUL'S USE OF THE TERM

Paul's use of the term *bema* and his references to rewards and wreath-crowns are parallel to the practice at the Panhellenic games. In his two uses of the word *bema* the subject is Christ's judgment of believers ("we"); he doesn't seem to have in mind a general judgment. Also, in two epistles where he discusses the subject of rewards such as the wreath-crowns, he compares the Christian life to a track meet and a boxing match, two major events in the games:

Do you not know that those who *run in a race* all run, but one receives the prize? Run in such a way that you may obtain it. And everyone who competes for the prize is temperate in all things. Now they do it to obtain a perishable crown, but we for an imperishable crown. Therefore I *run* thus: not with uncertainty. Thus, I *fight:* not as one who beats the air. But I discipline my body and bring it into subjection, lest, when I have preached to others, I myself should become disqualified. (1 Corinthians 9:24-27, italics added)

I have fought the good fight, I have finished the race, I have kept the faith. Finally, there is laid up for me the *crown of righteousness,* which the Lord, the righteous Judge, will give to me on that Day, and not to me only, but also to all who have loved His appearing. (2 Timothy 4:7-8, italics added)

We, like the Olympic athletes, need to avoid disqualification through moral compromise, and we need to compete to win! We, too, will stand before a judge at the end of our life's race. His name is Jesus, and many of us will win glorious, incorruptible wreath-crowns.

Hell and condemnation are not the issue here. The believer has already been legally judged at the cross. The *bema* is a time for evaluation and reward.

THE JUDGE

At the judgment seat our judgment has been placed into the hands of the ideal judge: the unique person of the universe, Jesus Christ (John 5:27; 2 Timothy 4:1). He is both undiminished deity and true, complete, glorified humanity. He has ultimate knowledge, perfect wisdom, and personal experience of living in this world. We are assured that His judgment will be perfectly just and true, not according to outward appearances (John 5:30; 7:24; 8:16; Romans 2:2, 3).

Since all judgment is His, when Paul teaches about the *bema,* he reminds us that there is no place for criticism between Christians: "Who are you to judge another's servant? To his own master he stands or falls. Indeed, he will be made to stand, for God is able to make him stand. . . . But why do you judge your brother? Or why do you show contempt for your brother? For we shall all stand before the judgment seat of Christ" (Romans 14:4, 10). For this same reason, the Christian is also exhorted not to seek vengeance (Hebrews 10:30; James 4:12; and Romans 12:17-21).

THE JUDGMENT PROCESS

First Corinthians 3:10-15 provides an expanded description of Christ's *bema* judgment:

> According to the grace of God which was given to me, as a wise master builder I have laid the foundation, and another builds on it. But let each one take heed how he builds on it. For no other foundation can anyone lay than that which is laid, which is Jesus Christ. Now if anyone builds on this foundation with gold, silver, precious stones, wood, hay, straw, each one's work will become manifest; for the Day will declare it, because it will be revealed by fire; and the fire will test each one's work, of what sort it is. If anyone's work which he has built on it endures, he will receive a reward. If anyone's work is burned, he will suffer loss; but he himself will be saved, yet so as through fire. (1 Corinthians 3:10-15)

After stating that the foundation for all meaningful ministry must be Christ, Paul lists the symbolic materials used to describe the various ways people try to build the church. The gold, silver, and precious stones are beautiful and most valuable. They will stand the test of the judgment seat of Christ.

However, the wood, hay, and straw are a different matter. Although our life ministries may appear to be substantial and lovely here on earth, the fiery eye of Jesus Christ will disclose their true value. Wood can look beautiful and be useful; hay has a definite but limited use; and straw has very limited use. However, all three serve only limited temporal purposes, having no lasting worth. Much that we do may have beauty and value on a totally human level. But does it have eternal value?

Paul describes the actual *bema* judgment in two steps. In the first step our lives are made manifest—all that we have ever done is revealed. The phrase "will become manifest" is a translation of the Greek word *phaneron,* which literally means to "open up" or "make manifest." This indicates that everything that we have done will be laid open and made completely public.

Luke 12:2-3 states that "there is nothing covered that will not be revealed, nor hidden that will not be known... whatever you have spoken in the dark will be heard in the light, and what you have spoken in the ear in inner rooms will be proclaimed on the housetops."

The second step is the testing of the value or worth of what has been exposed. That year that you taught in the primary Sunday school class—was that gold or was it wood? The year you spent changing diapers, feeling totally out of place and not really ministering—will that be the gold? What about those long hours and days you spent taking care of a bedridden loved one and not being able to participate in normal church activities? Or what of the time spent just talking and listening to your spouse, or the time you took your son fishing—were they not as precious stones in the eyes of Jesus?

The value of our ministry is based not on our limited human perspective but on what God considers to be truly valuable.

In the third step, once Jesus has openly displayed our lives and revealed the true value of all that is there, we are to receive rewards, assuming that something is left after the burning judgment of Christ. (Those with nothing left do not lose their salvation. Paul plainly states that the one with nothing is still saved, but as one who comes through a fire with nothing but his life.) The rewards that are then given include public commendation, a special entrance into the messianic Kingdom, wreath-crowns, and appointments to rule in the kingdom (Luke 12:8, 9; Matthew 25:21; Luke 19:17-26; 2 Peter 1:11).[6]

THE ISSUE OF WORKS

One of the more troubling aspects of the New Testament teaching on the *bema* is the importance of works. Some who teach on the *bema* suggest that salvation is for free, given by the grace of God, and that rewards at the *bema* are earned by works. This certainly seems to be what Paul is saying. In Ephesians 2:8-9, he declares that salvation is totally a gift of God's grace. Then, in 1 Corinthians 3:13-15 and 2 Corinthians 5:10 he repeatedly refers to the importance of works at the *bema* judgment.

On the other hand, Paul also clearly teaches that the way we begin the Christian life—that is, by faith—is the way we are to continue it (Colossians 2:6). He emphasizes that a law-works orientation in the Christian life is contrary to the work of the Spirit (Galatians 3:1-5; 5:1-26).

What is the resolution of this dilemma? I suggest that it centers in the nature of the New Testament teaching on grace-living. First, Paul indicates that works in the form of fruit are produced by the person who is walking in the Spirit (Galatians 5). Furthermore, Jesus taught in John 15:5 that all true fruit in our lives is ultimately produced by Him. He said, "For without me, you can do nothing."

Paradoxically, then, the person who on his own tries to produce good deeds in his life really has nothing of value to present to Jesus at the *bema*. On the other hand, the one who lives his Christian life as one author so aptly puts it, in a continual celebration of forgiveness, enjoying the freedom he has in Christ and focusing on abiding in a living, loving fellowship with Christ, will be able to present to Christ that which has eternal value.

We can conclude, therefore, that to prepare well for the *bema* primarily involves a walk of trusting obedience to God and His word, while enjoying a close, loving relationship with Jesus Christ. At the *bema* works will be but outward evidences of the reality of our walk with God.

Notes

1. In this basic sense Stephen describes Abraham as not even having possession of enough land for a step (*bema*) for his feet (Acts 7:5).

2. W. E. Vine, *An Expository Dictionary of New Testament Words*, 1966 ed., s.v. "Judgment-Seat."

3. This use is found in a number of places in the New Testament. The proconsuls Pilate, Galio, and Festus sat on *bemas* when they judged Jesus and Paul (Matthew 27:19; John 19:13; Acts 18:12, 16, 17; and Acts 25:6, 17). Likewise, King Herod and Caesar sat on *bemas* for their royal business (Acts 12:21; 25:10).

4. *Oxford Latin Dictionary*, ed. P. G. W. Glare (Oxford: At the Clarendon Press, 1982), pp. 447, 1971.

5. *Collier's Encyclopedia*, 1962 ed., s.v. "Olympic Games."

6. I recognize that the gospel passages mentioned were directed to Christ's disciples in the context of prechurch teaching. However, on three grounds I feel comfortable in applying the principles here to the Christian. First, the disciples became the foundation of the church, and these teachings were preparatory for their role in the church. Second, the gospels were addressed to and used first and only by the church, thus implying relevance to church-age believers. And finally, there is a good possibility that the judgment of believing Israelites will be a part of the event of the judgment seat of Christ.

4

The Christian's
After-Death Experience

There are two paths to the *bema* of Christ. One is through the rapture (the future time when all Christians are caught up to meet Jesus in the air at His second coming[1] and dead believers are resurrected). The second is through death. Because a serious consideration of the subject of death, and life after death, is a valuable context for understanding the coming *bema* of Christ, we will turn our attention to that normally much-avoided topic.

QUESTIONS ABOUT DEATH

My two boys and I packed our car, each step heavier than the last. This was not the normal, annual Christmas jaunt to Houston we eagerly looked forward to each year. It was very different. We were making our way home to await the death of my father-in-law, my sons' beloved "Gran."

Radiation had not worked; chemotherapy was too drastic for his frail body. As the boys and I walked into his house, the air reeked, not of Christmas cookies and joyful anticipation, but of resignation—resignation to mortality. Gran was dying.

Soon after we had unloaded the van, my mother-in-law told me that Gran wanted to visit with me alone as soon as I could. Everyone tried to make Gran comfortable in his lounge chair. Then the family left us alone. I opened the conversation, "Gran, what is it that you wanted to talk about?"

He replied, "Joe, would you tell me exactly what happens to a person when he dies?"

I was a bit surprised at his question. Here was a man who already knew much of what the Bible teaches about heaven and eternal life. He had been a deacon in his church and had taught Sunday school for many years. Yet, like many other Christians, he had never been taught many of the details about life after death. Now those truths were all very important to him.

Perhaps you, like Gran, want to know what God's Word says about what your after-death experience will be like.

THE DEATH EXPERIENCE

Both the reality and fear of death precipitate all sorts of questions and theories as to what death is really like.[2] What will happen to me when I die? Will I still exist as a person?

Will I have a body? If so, what will it be like? When does death actually occur? Can someone die, leave his body, and then return to his body?

NONSCRIPTURAL VIEWS

Materialists in our society argue that when we die everything ends. Man, they would say, is no different from the animal world. Many New Agers teach that after death we are reincarnated into other bodies, animal or human. Others have developed theories about our spirits' hovering for a time like ghosts over an area before departing to their eternal reward. In the Middle Ages the doctrine was developed that after death the Christian faced purgatory, a time when he would suffer for and be purged of sins that were not bad enough to require eternal damnation. In recent times, some cults have propounded a belief in soul sleep, the teaching that when we die our souls sleep in the body, awaiting the resurrection.

THE VIEW OF THE SCRIPTURES

The Scriptures have a different story to tell. First, the Scriptures clearly affirm that there definitely *is* life after death. Paul argued in 1 Corinthians 15 that if resurrection were not certain, then everything else about Christianity was false and Christians must deny the reality of what the gospel was actually doing in their lives.

Second, the proposed cycle of reincarnation that is widely taught throughout the various schools of eastern mysticism is impossible in light of the direct statement of Scripture: "It is appointed for men to die once, but after this the judgment" (Hebrews 9:27).

Third, it *is* possible to begin the death process and then return to life. In Scripture we find two types of resurrection —physical resuscitation and permanent resurrection. Christ's resurrection is called the "the firstfruits" from the grave, so it must be different from all earlier restorations to life in the Bible. In the Old Testament, for example, we have the accounts of Elijah's raising the son of the woman of Zarephath (1 Kings 17:17-24), the raising of the Shunammite's son by Elisha (2 Kings 4:18-37), and the resuscitation of the man buried in Elisha's tomb (2 Kings 4:20-21). In the New Testament both Christ and the apostles raised people from the dead: Lazarus (John 11), Jairus's daughter (Mark 5:35-43), the widow's son at Nain (Luke 7:11-16), Dorcas (Acts 9:36-42), and Eutychus (Acts 20:6-12).

Though all these persons were raised from the dead back to physical life, they experienced death a second time—to await the return of Christ and the resurrection at the rapture. By contrast, Jesus was raised permanently, never to die again. Thus we can designate Christ's resurrection as a *permanent resurrection,* whereas all others were merely *physical resuscitations.*

Make no mistake: Christ clearly died a "final physical death." Clear testimony of His true and final death was given when a spear was thrust in His side and blood and water poured out (John 19:34; 1 John 5:8-9).

The others obviously did not experience "final death." From a divine point of view Lazarus and Jairus's daughter were but asleep, as Jesus Himself specifically declared in His description of them (John 11:11-14 and Matthew 9:24). Similarly, Paul responded to the report that Eutychus was dead by stating that his life was still in him.[3]

It would appear, then, that though from a human viewpoint someone may seem "finally dead," from God's purpose and point of view his life may still be in him, because resuscitation is possible and imminent. And that in turn leads, as we have already seen, to the conclusion that all resurrections in the Bible and throughout history, except that of Jesus Christ Himself, have actually been physical resuscitations. Physical resuscitation is a form of resurrection, to be sure, as the physically dead are returned to physical life. But it is also quite different from both the resurrection of Christ and the resurrection we will experience. Those who have been physically restored to life have all died again, whereas Jesus rose from the dead never to die again, just as we will live with Him never to die again.

It seems then, that there are two stages in the dying process: first, the point at which a man's vital signs cease to exist, the point we might call "apparent death"; and second, the point at which God finally separates the soul and spirit from the body, which we might call "final death." Only God knows when the true line of final death is crossed. But when it is crossed, there is no turning back, as Scripture confirms in Hebrews 9:27.

OUT-OF-BODY EXPERIENCES

This distinction between reversible "apparent death" and irreversible "final death" opens the possibility for what many today refer to as "out-of-body" or "after-death" experiences. Generally I would agree with the conclusion John Weldon and Zola Levitt reach in their book *Is There Life After Death?*: that most of these supposed after-death experiences could well be the result of a natural trigger mechanism, such as extreme physiological stress or even anesthesia; and that others might be but fabrications, and still others the product of demonic counterfeits.[4]

However, in the light of the language and episodes of Scripture, a possibility exists that some people have moved beyond apparent, reversible death, but short of final death in their experiences, and have "come back" to tell about it. In fact, there is an account in Scripture of just such an experience. Paul wrote in 2 Corinthians 12: "I know a man in Christ who fourteen years ago—whether in the body I do not know, or whether out of the body I do not know, God knows—such a one was caught up to the third heaven. And I know such a man—whether in the body or out of the body I do not know, God knows—how he was caught up into Paradise and heard inexpressible words, which it is not lawful for a man to utter" (2 Corinthians 12:2-4).

Some interpreters believe Paul was speaking of someone other than himself, whereas others maintain that he was speaking of his own experience, possibly when he was stoned at Lystra and left for dead (Acts 14:19-20). In either case, Paul did voice at least the possibility of an "out-of-body experience." We may conclude then, that although many alleged after-death experiences can be explained clinically, there may be a percentage that fall into the category of Paul's out-of-body, near-final-death experience. Thus, someone who appears to be dead from the human perspective may be just going through a near-final-death experience.

We do have a clear statement in Hebrews 9:27, however, that when a person truly and finally dies, he irreversibly faces divine judgment. All other experiences are merely forms of pre-final death. The time of a person's final, irreversible death is determined by the will of God alone.

AFTER WE DIE, WHAT THEN?

Scripture does not support any concept of purgatory, and it directly contradicts any thought of soul sleep. Rather it states that when the Christian is absent from the physical body at permanent death he is present with the Lord. Here is Paul's way of describing what happens when we die:

Knowing that He who raised up the Lord Jesus will also raise us up with Jesus and will present us with you. For all things are for your sakes, that grace, having spread through the many, may cause thanksgiving to abound to the glory of God. Therefore we do not lose heart. Even though our outward man is perishing, yet the inward man is being renewed day by day. For our light affliction, which is but for a moment, is working for us a far more exceeding and eternal weight of glory, while we do not look at the things which are seen, but at the things which are not seen. For the things which are seen are temporary, but the things which are not seen are eternal.

For we know that if our earthly house, this tent, is destroyed, we have a building from God, a house not made with hands eternal in the heavens. For indeed in this we groan, earnestly desiring to be clothed with our habitation which is from heaven. if indeed, having been clothed, we shall not be found naked. For indeed while we who are in this tent groan, being burdened, not because we want to be unclothed, but further clothed, that mortality may be swallowed up by life. Now He who has prepared us for this very thing is God, who also has given us the Spirit as a guarantee. Therefore we are always confident, knowing that while we are at home in the body we are absent from the Lord. For we walk by faith, not by sight. We are confident, yes, well pleased rather to be absent from the body and to be present with the Lord. Therefore we make it our aim, whether present or absent, to be well pleasing to Him. For we must all appear before the judgment seat of Christ, that each one may receive the things done in the body, according to what he has done, whether good or bad. (2 Corinthians 4:14–5:10)

AN INTERMEDIATE BODY

This passage is interpreted in four major ways. Lewis Sperry Chafer taught that the passage describes an intermediate body that clothes the believer's soul when he dies and in which he will wait for the rapture.[5] In this view, the believer will receive his eternal, glorified body later at the rapture, along with those who are living believers, and then he will be judged at the *bema*.

Such an interpretation requires a distinction between the eternal house in verse 1 and the habitation in verse 2, since the new house in 2 Corinthians 5:1 is eternal, not temporary, as an intermediate body would need to be. However, the introduction of an intermediate body in verse 2 does not appear to fit into the flow of Paul's argument. The eternal house in verse 1 is from God and the habitation in verse 2 is from heaven, thus implying, without any further explanation, that they are the same thing.

A RESURRECTION BODY

A second interpretation is proposed by C. K. Barrett in his commentary on 2 Corinthians.[6] He interprets the passage as saying that Paul had the resurrection body in view. The word *have* in verse 1, he says, is a prophetic present, looking forward to what we will have when Jesus comes back. The rest of Paul's discussion, then, is the expression of his desire to live all the way to the rapture and thus not die and be found a naked soul.

There are a number of problems with this view. First, Paul's hope of not dying and making it to the resurrection is not the subject of the immediately preceding context. Paul is talking about his body moving toward death. Second, the passage is concerned with what happens when we are absent from the body, i.e., dead. Third, at no point in this passage is that which clothes us in the future called a body. The term *body* is used only of the physical body; house terms are used with regard to the future. Thus the passage is not talking about the future, glorified, resurrected body at all. Finally, saying that the passage is speaking of a future, glorified, resurrected body fails to do justice to the clear statement of Paul that his explanations in 2 Corinthians 5 are the basis for his not "losing heart" in the face of a body that is on its way to death.

NO SEPARATION BETWEEN THE POINT OF
DEATH AND THE RESURRECTION

A third interpretation has been made by Ray Stedman.[7] He suggests that when we leave the body we leave time. So at death, when we enter eternity there is no separation between the point of death and the resurrection, assuming we are spiritually prepared to receive the resurrection body.

This scenario is possible, I suppose. However, such a concept is not explicitly taught in Scripture. Also it forces us to eliminate the possibility of the sequence of events in eternity, which seems to be contradicted by the presence in the book of Revelation by stated sequences of events in heaven. Furthermore, the absence of the sequence of events in Stedman's interpretation seems to make eternity less than a fully real, personal existence.

A GLORIOUS HEAVENLY HOME "OVERCLOTHING" THE BELIEVER

Finally, there is the position espoused by Charles Hodge.[8] Hodge suggested that the hope Paul expected joyously at the point of death when he left his physical body (tabernacle) behind was not a different body at all, but rather his new home in heaven, where, without a resurrected body, he would be "overclothed" with his glorious heavenly habitation. Though he would not yet have his resurrection body, he would not be found naked, because he would be surrounded by the glory of his heavenly home.

This view has much to commend it. It agrees with the argument of the passage, namely that we don't lose heart in the face of death because of the wonderful expectation we have when we die: a glorious heavenly home and being present with Christ. Also it recognizes the differences in the terms used by Paul to describe being clothed (i.e., whenever the heavenly house is referred to, he uses the term "overclothed," as an outer garment being put over another; whereas when he refers to the physical body, he uses the simple terms "clothed" or "unclothed"). Finally, the term "overclothed" is a most appropriate way to describe a heavenly house covering us. Now let me paraphrase the argument that this interpretation assumes:

We don't lose heart, though our physical bodies are on their way to death. You need to understand that our present troubles are nothing compared to the heavy weight of glory that bearing up under suffering produces for the future in heaven. So our focus is on these future unseen eternal things (4:16-18).

Here's why we feel this way:

(1) If our earthly house, which is really a temporary tabernacle, is taken down (i.e., we die), then we know that we have a building in heaven that is our permanent dwelling place (5:1).

(2) In addition, in this tabernacle (our physical body) we are groaning and desiring that the dwelling place we are intended to inhabit might overclothe us so that—and I am certainly assuming it to be the case—when we are unclothed our estate might not be that of a naked soul (since the eternal weight of glory and an eternal house await us; 5:2-3).

(3) In addition, we who are in the tabernacle are groaning because of the heavy weight we have both in the form of burdens now and glory in the future. Because of this, we do not want to be unclothed, but overclothed (i.e., have the glory of the heavenly house cover us). And our groaning is for the experience that the frail, human mortality might be swallowed up by the life that Jesus has already begun in us (5:4; see 4:10-11).

And parenthetically we can be assured of all of this because we know that God has prepared us for this and has already given us the pledge of the Holy Spirit (5:5).

Therefore, all of this gives us confidence as we move toward death; and besides, we also are not only confident but even well pleased to die and be absent from the body, because such a condition means that we are present with the Lord (5:6-8).

The conclusion of the matter: (1) since physical life is temporary, that is, since all of us will have an end to our physical existence (whether we are still present in our physical bodies when Christ comes, or we are absent and already in heaven); and (2) since all of us, whether we are dead or living when Jesus comes back, will have to appear before Christ's *bema* (judgment seat), whatever we do, we want to live in a way that is well pleasing to Him (5:9-10).

Paul is not making a contrast between our earthly bodies and our resurrection bodies; he is contrasting earth and heaven. Assuming this, there are a number of relevant conclusions about death we can draw from the passage:

1. When we die, we go directly to heaven. (See also Philippians 1:21.)
2. In heaven we are wondrously in the presence of Christ.
3. Some of our rewards await us in the form of glory in our heavenly habitation right after we die.
4. What comes after death is not to be feared, but longed for.
5. Our glorious, eternal body awaits the resurrection from the dead at the coming of Christ—this is corroborated by such passages as 1 Corinthians 15.
6. The focus of our expectation of death should be to prepare for the *bema* of Christ.

THE RESURRECTION

There is more to come. Not only will we be "overclothed" with our glorious heavenly habitation and present with the Lord at death, but when Jesus again returns for His church at the time of the rapture our bodies will be raised from the dead as eternal, glorified bodies.[9]

What will these glorified bodies be like? In his letter to the Philippians, Paul states:

> For our citizenship is in heaven, from which we also eagerly wait for the Savior, the Lord Jesus Christ, who will transform our lowly body that it may be *conformed to His glorious body*, according to the working by which He is able even to subdue all things to Himself. (Philippians 3:20-21, italics added)

And John says:

> Beloved, now we are children of God; and it has not yet been revealed what we shall be, but we know that when He is revealed, *we shall be like Him,* for we shall see Him as He is. (1 John 3:2, italics added)

When we see Jesus, we will become like Him. Of course, we will not share in His total glorification as deity, but we will be given bodies with the characteristics of His glorified humanity.

After His resurrection, Jesus had a real body, similar in some respects to His precrucifixion body. Though it was not physical, He could be seen when He wanted to be seen (Luke 24:13-32), and He could be touched and felt (Luke 24:39). Though there is no mention of any blood, Jesus said that His body had flesh and bone (Luke 24:39). He could eat, even though apparently He did not have to eat (Luke 24:41-43). He was not limited by time, space, or substance (Luke 24:36).

We, too, will not be limited by the material world, and we will have bodies that are capable of eating and are recognizable to others. Our bodies then will be similar to the physical bodies we had before death, yet qualitatively far superior.

What will we look like? What age will we appear to be? What about babies or unborn children? Will they be babies throughout eternity? Probably the answer to those questions again lies in considering the resurrection body of Jesus. If we will be like Jesus, perhaps the Scriptures are telling us that we will appear as we did, or might have appeared to be, at the age of our physical maturity, but without the blemishes caused by personal sin and the sin of the race.

Also remember that after His death and resurrection and at the time of His coming again Jesus still had, and will retain, the scars of His crucifixion (John 20:25-27; Zechariah 12:10). Apparently scars that are the result of suffering for God will remain in our bodies in some form, not as terrible blemishes but as eternal badges of honor that bring continuous glory to God. I would think then that our eternal bodies will retain only those scars that were a part of "filling up the sufferings of Jesus" (Colossians 1:24), and that they will serve as eternal reminders of our love and loyalty to Christ.

According to 1 Corinthians 15:35-54, our resurrection bodies will be similar to our earthly physical bodies. This implies that we will be recognizable. This passage also says that we will be raised in "glory, incorruption, and power." We will have bodies that cannot die but are capable of judging over angels (1 Corinthians 6:3) as we reassume our rightful role as rulers over the creation (Psalm 8; Hebrews 2:5-10; Romans 8:17).

The thirteenth chapter of 1 Corinthians adds this point: "we will know just as we are also known." The total extent of this knowledge is not clear, but certainly we will be able to see ourselves as God sees us and will understand finally the meaning and purpose of all that has happened in our lives. Perhaps we will even be able to move back through time and view the events of history from God's perspective and have all the "whys" explained to us.

Further, Paul in Ephesians tells us that when we appear in His presence we will be pure and spotless, apparently without sin (Ephesians 5:25-27).

Revelation 21:4 assures us that our glorified bodies will never die and that at some point, even though we still experience emotions, God will wipe away all tears and end all sorrow and pain.

Instead of the "sting of death," we will experience only victory; we will have bodies that are real; we will still feel emotion; we will be able to eat; we will not be hindered by physical limitations; we will be pure and sinless; we will never die or get sick; and we will be with Christ as He rules over the entire creation.

THE *BEMA* AND BEYOND

Then with our resurrected bodies we will appear in the holy presence of Jesus at His judgment seat. Following our examination by Jesus and the granting of rewards, there will be a great wedding and feast for the Lamb of God, Jesus Christ, and His bride, the church. This feast will either take place in heaven immediately prior to the second advent of Christ or it will be announced at that time and take place right after the second advent and Jesus' triumphal entry into Jerusalem and the establishment of the messianic kingdom. Some suggest that the millennial stage of the kingdom is actually one thousand years of celebration of the marriage of the Lamb. See Revelation 19:7-21:2 for this description.

Then, either after or contemporaneous with the marriage of the Lamb, believers are ushered into the kingdom and established in their places of honor and responsibility.

SUMMARY OF OUR AFTER-DEATH EXPERIENCE

In this chapter we have discussed much about what we are to expect as Christians when we die. Therefore, it may be helpful to review a digest of what we have learned so far:

1. We will either die or be raptured (Hebrews 9:27; 1 Thessalonians 4:13-18).

2. When we die, we are ushered immediately into the glorious presence of the living God and receive our eternal habitation, where we await the rapture and the resurrection of our bodies (2 Corinthians 5:8).

3. Later, our dead bodies are resurrected, are reformed by the power of God, and become eternal, glorified bodies like Christ's glorious body (John 3:2; Philippians 3:20-21).

4. We then appear before the judgment seat (*bema*) of Christ. Each of our lives will be an open book. Our deeds and our thoughts will be made evident along with our motives (1 Corinthians 3:13; 4:5). Some of us will be ashamed (1 John 2:28).

5. The quality of each person's work will be examined by the fiery eyes of Christ, and all that is sinful or worthless will be burned away (1 Corinthians 3:13-15).

6. Rewards will be given and honors bestowed (1 Corinthians 3:14).

7. The marriage of the Lamb of God, Jesus Christ, to His bride, the church (who is now clothed in the beauty of

her righteous acts), will take place (with its festive celebration) either in heaven before, or on the earth after, the triumphal second advent (Revelation 19-21).

8. Finally, after we enter the kingdom triumphantly with the King of Kings, we are appointed to our places of honor and responsibility in the glorious messianic kingdom (Matthew 25:34).

Notes

1. I believe that the second coming is in two phases, the *rapture,* during which living Christians, Christians who have already died, and possibly Old Testament believers are caught up to meet the Lord in the air; and the *triumphal return of Christ* at the close of the Tribulation but before the Millennium. Not all Christians hold to this view concerning the nature of the second coming. See chapter 6 (and especially endnotes 1-3) for a more thorough discussion of this subject.

   In this book we are addressing what happens to a Christian who dies before Jesus comes back at the time of the rapture of the church. There are a variety of opinions among Christians as to the resurrection of Old Testament believers and people who are saved during the Tribulation. First Corinthians 15:23 indicates that people will be resurrected in a planned order. Apparently Old Testament believers are resurrected with the church-age saints at the time of the rapture and the Tribulation saints are raised at the triumphal return of Christ. Some suggest, however, that the Old Testament saints have already been raised. They point to Matthew's statement in Matthew 27:52-53, where it is said that people saw Old Testament saints alive from the dead after Jesus had been raised. Not much else is said, so this might only be a temporary resuscitation. Revelation 20 tells us of the resurrection of unbelievers at the end of the millennial kingdom period in preparation for the great white throne judgment.

2. The term *death* is used in Scripture in at least seven different ways:
   (1) Physical death (Genesis 5, and elsewhere)
   (2) Spiritual death—separation from God's life and fellowship with him (Genesis 2:17; Romans 6:23; Ephesians 2:1)
   (3) Second death—in the lake of fire (Revelation 20:14)
   (4) Positional death of the believer—by being in Christ, he is seen by God as already dead by crucifixion along with Christ (Romans 6:3-8)
   (5) Sexual death—being beyond the time of being able to bear children (Romans 4:19)
   (6) Temporal spiritual death—not living as Christians in touch with the life of Christ (Ephesians 5:14)
   (7) Dying to selfish desires (John 12:24)

3. Admittedly the reference to sleep in these passages is not conclusive support by itself of this view, for the death of believers awaiting the rapture is called sleep in 1 Thessalonians. Nevertheless, it is possible that Jesus' use of the term *sleep* in the context of other statements about the person in question being dead was meant to leave the impression that Jesus was about to arouse the dead person, as from sleep, not to bring him back from paradise with a life in him that would never die. In any case,

there is ample evidence for different kinds of deaths and resurrections, for the kind of body Lazarus and Jairus's daughter had after being raised was different from the kind of body Jesus had after the resurrection. Also, Hebrews clearly states that when one is truly and finally dead, it only happens once and is followed by the judgment (Hebrews 9:27).

4. John Weldon and Zola Levitt, *Is There Life After Death?* (Irvine, Calif.: Harvest, 1977), p. 52.

5. Lewis Sperry Chafer, *Systematic Theology*, 8 vols. (Dallas: Dallas Theological Seminary Press, 1957), 4:414-15.

6. C. K. Barrett, *A Commentary of the Second Epistle to the Corinthians* (New York: Harper & Row, 1973), pp. 149-61.

7. Ray C. Stedman, *Expository Studies in 2 Corinthians: Power Out of Weakness* (Waco, Tex.: Word), pp. 94-95.

8. Charles Hodge, *An Exposition of the Second Epistle to the Corinthians* (Grand Rapids: Eerdmans, 1973), pp. 106-28.

9. See note 1 for further discussion of this subject.

5

Our Heavenly Habitations

If you observe the media as much as I do, hardly a week goes by that you do not see either in print or on television some kind of misrepresentation of what heaven really is. We've all seen the cartoons picturing winged people sitting on clouds and strumming harps. Even many Christians speak of heaven as some kind of ethereal otherworld where nothing is real and where one dwells in blissful ignorance and anonymity. If people commonly speak of heaven as a place far off in the sky—where we rest on clouds, dressed in white and playing little hand-held harps, day in and day out, forever—is it any wonder that many of us do not long for the day we enter heaven? The truth is, we desperately need an awareness of the reality of heaven as it is revealed in Scripture if we are to correctly understand all that happens after we die and all that concerns the judgment seat of Christ and heavenly rewards. Heaven is not a cartoon kingdom or a whimsical fantasyland. It is a real place. It is where the throne room of our majestic Creator is established and exists right now, today, even as you read the words of this page.

THE THREE HEAVENS

The Old Testament word for heaven (*shamayim*) comes from a root word meaning "to be high or lofty."[1] The New Testament word is *ouranos*. It is used in classical Greek to refer to the arch or vault of heaven over the earth.[2] Both terms are used to refer to three different heavens.

The first heaven is *the atmospheric heaven,* the place where birds fly and clouds bring rain. The second heaven is *the celestial* or *starry heaven.* This is the vast universe of stars and planets that appear to us to be virtually limitless. Often the Bible relates the angelic creation to this heaven. Both the angels and the stars are called the "host of heaven," and angels in Job 38:7 are called "singing stars." The Scriptures leave the impression that the physical universe is inhabited, inhabited by various kinds of creatures all of whom we know as messengers or angels (both the Hebrew and Greek words for angel literally mean messenger). The third heaven is *the dwelling place of God,* the place where believers go at death, where Jesus sits at the right hand of the Father, and where we will one day be present with the Lord.

What is our relationship to each of these heavens? The first heaven—the atmosphere—is simply a vehicle that makes possible the existence of life on earth and does not greatly concern our study here. The second heaven will be remade when God makes all things new (Revelation 21:5). Isaiah the prophet says that the renovation will begin with the Tribulation period (Isaiah 24) and that both the heavens and the earth will be made new at the beginning of the millennial kingdom (Isaiah 65:17-25). At the end of the Millennium and after the great white throne judgment the heavenly city from the third heaven will descend to the newly renovated earth and the "new heavens and the new earth" will finally be complete (Revelation 21:1-4). Believers will live forever in this renovated heaven and remade earth, and they will reign with Christ over the eternal new heavens and new earth, just as they reigned with Him over the millennial kingdom (Revelation 1:6).

A Closer Look at Heaven

The Bible describes the third heaven, the dwelling place of God and the center of our eternal existence after we die, in three major ways.

THE TABERNACLE AND THE TEMPLE

The epistle to the Hebrews says that the Tabernacle of ancient Israel and the priestly services were "a copy and shadow of the heavenly things" and that Moses "was divinely instructed when he was about to make the tabernacle" (Hebrews 8:5). Thus it appears that not only was it that God gave Moses the pattern for the Tabernacle, the pattern He gave to Moses was a copy of the way things are in heaven. A similar situation occurs in the descriptions of heaven in the book of Revelation. The apostle John described heaven in the book of Revelation with terms taken straight from descriptions of Israel's Tabernacle and its later counterpart, the Temple.

In the Revelation, Jesus is symbolically dressed as a *priestly* judge in the midst of *golden lampstands.* From under the *altar* martyrs appeal to God for divine justice (6:9). *Incense* ascends from the *golden altar* in heaven, and the coals from that *altar* carry judgment to the earth (8:3-5). This same *altar* is referred to again in 9:13 and 16:7. The Tribulation martyrs serve God in the *Temple* (7:15) of heaven and God spreads "His *tabernacle* over" His people (7:15, italics added; NASB*). There are thirteen additional references to the heavenly Temple in Revelation. In Revelation 13:5-6, when the Antichrist blasphemes God, he also blasphemes God's *Tabernacle* and those who are *tabernacled* in heaven.

Heaven, therefore, must look much like the Tabernacle and the Temple in the Old Testament. So a brief survey of what the Tabernacle was like will reveal much about what heaven is like.

The Tabernacle was Israel's worship center. There the people met with Yahveh, their God. It was divided into three parts:

(1) *The Court:* The court was the area inside a linen fence and outside the covered, holy building. In the court were two articles of furniture: the brazen altar of burnt offering and the brazen laver for washing.

New American Standard Bible.

(2) *The Holy Place:* The main part of the Tabernacle was a roofless, gold-covered, wooden building, set up under a large, four-layer tent. The front part of this gold-covered, wooden building was called the Holy Place. In the Holy Place were three articles of furniture: the table of showbread, the seven-lamp lampstand, and the golden altar of incense.

(3) *The Holy of Holies:* The Holy of Holies was located in the innermost part of the gold-covered, wooden building and under a four-layer tent. This part of the Tabernacle was separated from the Holy Place by a great veil. Behind the veil was a gold-covered, wooden box containing the stone tablets of the Ten Commandments. This box was called the Ark of the Covenant. On top of this Ark was a golden lid called the mercy seat; fastened to it were two golden cherubs. It was here, above the cherubs, that God revealed His glorious presence among His people: the "shekinah"[3] glory.

We may infer a number of things about heaven from this design. In heaven God has a throne room with a manifestation of His presence above some cherubs and separated from those who dwell in heaven by something like a great veil. Most likely, then, the heavenly Holy Place is where dead believers live, possibly the same as the "paradise" and "Abraham's bosom" mentioned in other passages (Luke 16:22; 23:43).

The court of the Tabernacle probably represents earth and the rest of the physical universe, and the brazen altar of sacrifice in the Tabernacle probably represents the cross where Jesus, the Lamb of God, was sacrificed (Hebrews 9:11-28).

At the completion of Jesus' sacrifice on the cross, God ripped the veil in the Temple in Jerusalem in two, from top to bottom. We can infer from this that the heavenly veil also was split open, so that all pre-cross believers now have full access into the very presence of God. If that is the case, then apparently those dead believers needed the application of the cleansing blood sacrifice of Christ before they could gain access to God (Hebrews 9:23). Perhaps Jesus had that heavenly cleansing in mind when He told the disciples He was departing so that He could prepare a place for them (John 14:1-3).

Heaven is also described in Scripture through the visions of the prophets. Ezekiel saw four great cherubs with wheels below a great throne. On the throne was an awesome, fiery revelation of the Lord:

> Then I looked, and, behold, a whirlwind came out of the north, a great cloud, with raging fire engulfing itself, and a brightness was all around it, and radiating out of its midst like the color of amber, out of the midst of the fire.
>
> Also from within it came the likeness of four living creatures. And this was their appearance; they had the likeness of a man. Each one had four faces, and each one had four wings. . . . The likeness of the firmament above the heads of the living creatures was like the color of an awesome crystal, stretched out over their heads. And under the firmament their wings spread out straight, one toward another. Each one had two, which covered one side, and each one had two which covered the other side of the body. When they went, I heard the noise of their wings, like the noise of great waters, like the voice of the Almighty, a tumult like the noise of an army; . . . And above the firmament over their heads was the likeness of a throne, in appearance like a sapphire stone; on the likeness of the throne was a likeness with the appearance of a man high above it. Also from the appearance of His waist and upward I saw, as it were, the color of amber with the appearance of fire all around within it; and from the appearance of His waist and downward I saw, as it were, the appearance of fire with brightness all around. Like the appearance of a rainbow in a cloud on a rainy day, so was the appearance of the brightness all around it. This was the appearance of the likeness of the glory of the Lord. So when I saw it, I fell on my face. (Ezekiel 1:4-6, 22-24, 26-28*a*)

Daniel, too, saw the fiery throne of God, with its wheels, and the awesome revelation of the "Ancient of Days" on the throne (Daniel 7:9-10). The apostle John saw the throne room of God as similar to what Ezekiel and Daniel saw (Revelation 4:1-11).

THE HEAVENLY JERUSALEM

The third major way heaven is pictured in Scripture is as a great city inhabited by the bride of Christ: the heavenly Jerusalem. In the New Jerusalem God dwells with His people; He wipes away all tears; He ends death, sorrow, crying, and pain. The city is a glorious one, into which no evil may enter. There is no night there, and no need of the sun or of lights, for the Lord God gives all the light that is needed.

That is what the third heaven is like. It will be our eternal home. But we will also have a direct relationship with the rest of the universe. In the messianic kingdom of Messiah Jesus, the whole creation will be remade, and the atmospheric and celestial heavens will likewise be a part of Jesus' eternal kingdom, and we will certainly have access to enjoy the entirety of the creation. Our place and responsibility in this new creation will be determined by the focal event of life after death, the *bema* of Christ.

QUESTIONS MOST OFTEN ASKED ABOUT HEAVEN AND LIFE AFTER DEATH

People have asked me a number of questions about heaven and life after death. Here are some of them:

1. *Can a person who has died observe us?*

We have no clear evidence that dead people can actually observe us. Some teach that Hebrews 12:1 supports the notion that we are being observed by dead believers: "Therefore we also, since we are surrounded by so great a cloud of witnesses." However, those witnesses are the ones referred to in chapter 11, and it is their lives and testimonies that witness to us that we should persevere in faith. The only ones that the Bible clearly says are observing us besides God are the angels (1 Corinthians 11:10).

2. *Can we communicate with the dead?*

The Bible warns us against trying to communicate with the dead, as it makes us vulnerable to lying spirits familiar with the lives of our dead loved ones (Deuteronomy 18:9-14).

3. *What happens to a person who commits suicide?*

He doesn't have time to deal with the sin he is committing before he dies. All of our sins were paid for at the cross, including sins like suicide. Therefore, a Christian who commits suicide does not face hell. However, he does have to face the *bema* with the shame of such a sin and will certainly receive stern reproof from Christ and miss certain rewards reserved for those who finish their courses.

4. *Will we experience the same relationships that we have in life now, such as marriage and parenthood? Will we know the pain of separation from loved ones who did not know Jesus' saving power?*

Jesus said that in heaven we will be like the angels of heaven, neither marrying nor being given in marriage (Matthew 22:30). Revelation 21 says that Jesus will wipe away all tears and remove all pain. Also, on a number of occasions the prophets comforted Israel with the assurance that in the messianic kingdom their relationship with the Lord would be so wonderful they would forget old relationships and pain from the past (Isaiah 43:18,19; 54:4-8). I believe that church age believers will be given similar blessings in the kingdom.

5. *How can heaven be a place of joy if I am aware of loved ones who are not there?*

First, ultimately the joy of heaven is in our complete and unending fellowship with God—the joy of the Lord. Because of the wonder of experiencing the greatness of God's love and glorious light, it will be difficult to remember much from the past that did not include Him. Second, once we are in heaven we will know even as we are known (1 Corinthians 13:12). Such knowledge may well provide a different view of those with whom we had past relationships but who were not part of the family of God. We will clearly see the reality of their depravity and rebellion against God and His love, and their part in the family of the enemy of our souls.

6. *What will we do in heaven?*

The Bible does not tell us much about activities in heaven, but the picture seems to be far from boredom. Not only will we dwell in heaven in the presence of the eternal, omnipotent Lord of the universe but we will have access to and rule with other believers over the recreated heavens and earth. We will be given responsibilities, and we will experience great knowledge, power, and joy. We will live eternally, with no pain or fear of death, and will participate in reunions and the joy of discovery, always with the continual ecstatic experience of worship in the very presence of our blessed Lord Jesus Christ. In some ways it will be a restored paradise, Eden revisited.

7. *How will I enjoy eternity, if I do not receive great rewards at the* bema?

Again, the joy of eternity is in our eternal relationship with our lovely Lord Jesus. I believe it will be somewhat like college graduation. Some have greater joy because of greater awards, but all of the graduates rejoice in the fact that they have graduated, and they also rejoice in the honors given to their friends. In heaven we will certainly see each other without jealousy and will rejoice in each other's blessings.

These few responses to questions about life after death and heaven are but suggestions in the light of biblical revelation we have on the subject. It is transparently clear that heaven will be a place of eternal joy that no memory can hinder.

Notes

1. Francis Brown, S. R. Driver, and Charles A. Briggs, *A Hebrew and English Lexicon of the Old Testament* (Oxford: Clarendon Press, 1959), p. 1029.
2. *Theological Dictionary of the New Testament*, 1968 ed., s.v. "*Ouranos.*"
3. The word *shekinah* means "resident." God's glory can be seen in many different forms and places, but He also manifests His glorious presence in a particular place. When that takes place, His glory is said to be a *shekinah*, or resident.

6

Prophecy and the *Bema*

As the twentieth century fades into history, radical changes in international affairs make the headlines almost daily. Historians and political analysts are stunned by unexpected events, and politicians hastily structure new paradigms for global relations.

Some suggest that we are witnessing significant signs that point to the soon return of our Lord Jesus Christ. If this is true, the judgment seat (*bema*) of Christ may also take place very soon. This prospect ought to compel us to watch seriously the way we live. We just might be interrupted right in the middle of some shameful or worthless activity to appear in the presence of Jesus—to be evaluated at the *bema*.

UNDERSTANDING THE MAJOR EVENTS IN PROPHECY

If we are to grasp the relevance of current events to biblical prophecy in general, and the *bema* in particular, we need to understand the basic prophetic order of events for the history of the planet.

THE TRIBULATION PERIOD

The Old Testament prophets, the apostles, and Jesus Himself all describe a seven-year period of divine judgment for the world. This period is known by many names: "the time of the indignation," "the time of Jacob's trouble," "the seventieth week of Daniel," and "the Day of the Lord." Jesus describes the last three and a half years of this period as the "Great Tribulation" (Matthew 24). Today, Bible teachers commonly refer to the entire period of seven years as the "Tribulation period."

Figure 1
The Tribulation Period

THE CHURCH AGE	TRIBULATION
Present	7 Years

Scripture verses that especially pertain to this period are Deuteronomy 4:30,31; Isaiah 2:19; 24:1-6, 19-20; 26:20, 21; Jeremiah 30:7; Daniel 12:2; Matthew 24:15-22; 1 Thessalonians 5:3; and Revelation 6:15-17.

THE MESSIANIC KINGDOM

Both the Old and New Testaments agree that Jesus, the Messiah, will return to the earth at the close of the Tribulation period to introduce His messianic kingdom, an eternal kingdom of peace, prosperity, and justice. The first phase of His kingdom is called the Millennium (from the Latin word for one thousand, *millennium*) because it will last one thousand years.[1] During this time, Jesus will demonstrate how world history could have been, had earthly rulers chosen to submit totally to God as sovereign.

At the end of the Millennium Jesus will judge all unbelievers. Revelation 20:11 says that Jesus will sit on a great white throne and carry out this final judgment. Then follows the second phase of the messianic kingdom, often referred to as the "Eternal State." In this phase all believers will enjoy the blessing of ruling for all eternity with Christ over the entire creation in a universe unblemished by sin.

Figure 2
The Millennium in Relation to the Tribulation

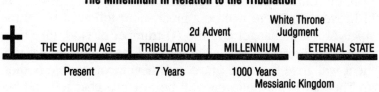

Scripture verses that especially pertain to this period are 2 Samuel 7; Psalm 2; 89; 110; Isaiah 2; 11; 35; Zechariah 14; and Revelation 20.

THE SECOND COMING OF CHRIST

The second coming of Christ will be in two phases: first the rapture, then the second advent.

The rapture,[2] the first phase of the second coming, is a special event for the church that God chose not to disclose until the writing of the New Testament. At the rapture, Christ will remove all believers—the church—from the world and then return to heaven for a time.

The second phase of the second coming, the second advent, will occur at the end of the Tribulation period, when Christ again returns to dwell on the earth. At this coming Jesus will deliver Israel and defeat the Antichrist and his great army at the Battle of Armageddon in Palestine. He then will judge the nations and establish His throne for rule in the millennial kingdom. Scripture verses that especially pertain to this period are Matthew 24; 1 Thessalonians 4; 5; 2 Thessalonians 1:2; and Revelation 19.

MORE ABOUT THE RAPTURE

The rapture is described or referred to in 1 Corinthians 15, in every chapter of 1 Thessalonians, and in chapter 2 of 2 Thessalonians. The fullest description is found in 1 Thessalonians 4:13-18. There Paul reveals seven specific details concerning the rapture.

At the rapture (1) Jesus Christ (not an intermediary or vision, but Christ Himself in His glorified body) will appear out of heaven. (2) There will be a great shout followed by (3) the voice of the archangel and the (4) trumpet of God. (5) Those who knew Christ as Savior but are no longer alive at that moment will arise from the grave with new incorruptible bodies. (6) Then all living believers will be instantly changed and become immortal. Finally, (7) both groups will be caught up into the clouds to meet Jesus (1 Thessalonians 4:13-18).

Although Scripture is fairly detailed about this event, some have inferred certain conclusions that may or may not be true. For instance, the Scriptures teach that the rapture is a mystery (or "secret," 1 Corinthians 15:5) and that believers will be changed "in the twinkling of an eye" (1 Corinthians 15:52). Some deduce from this that we all will vanish instantly and leave the world secretly at the rapture.

That conclusion, though possible, is not required by the biblical evidence. Those who teach this fail to recognize that the *change* is said to be instantaneous, not the *departure* itself. Furthermore, the Greek word *musterion,* which is translated "mystery" in 1 Corinthians 15:5, really refers to a truth that was a secret in the past (i.e., in Old Testament times) but is now revealed to the church. We do not know for certain, but it is even possible that we might be changed instantly, but remain visible. Our departure may even allow time to land airplanes and stop automobiles, and even have time to wave at others as we rise into the sky—all after we have experienced the instantaneous change.

Of even more significance is the lack of information about the precise time the rapture will take place. Scripture does not dictate that any specific prophetic event must precede the rapture. We are told, however, that the rapture "delivers us from the wrath to come" (1 Thessalonians 1:10), so we should expect the rapture to precede the wrath of the Tribulation period (Matthew 24:15; Revelation 6:17).[3] Thus we are left with the impression that date setting is futile, and that Jesus does not have to wait until the events in the Tribulation period take place before He comes for His church.

Paul repeatedly exhorts us to focus on Jesus' return, and we are encouraged to "love His appearing" and to "prepare," not for the Tribulation period, but for Christ's return for us. Thus the strong implication is that we are to live as though our Lord could come back today, and we are to be ready to face Him (1 Thessalonians 1:10; 2:19; 3:12,13; 5:1-11; 2 Timothy 4:8).

Figure 3
The Rapture in Relation to the Millennium and the Church Age

	Rapture	2d Advent	White Throne Judgment	
THE CHURCH AGE	TRIBULATION	MILLENNIUM		ETERNAL STATE
Present	7 Years	1000 Years Messianic Kingdom		

THE *BEMA*

The last part of the prophetic overview we are undertaking is the *bema* itself (2 Corinthians 5:10; Romans 14:10). According to Scripture, the *bema* evaluation will take place in heaven following the rapture. While angels are dispensing God's holy wrath onto the earth during the Tribulation period, Jesus will be conducting His *bema* judgment in heaven. Dwight Pentecost aptly presents the evidence pointing to the time of the *bema*:

> *The time of the* bema *of Christ.* The event herein described takes place immediately following the translation of the church out of this earth's sphere. There are several considerations that support this. (1) In the first place, according to Luke 14:14, reward is associated with the resurrection. Since, according to 1 Thessalonians 4:13-17, the resurrection is an integral part of the translation, reward must be a part of that program. (2) When the Lord returns to the earth with His bride to reign, the bride is seen to be already rewarded. This is observed in Revelation 19:7, where it must be observed that the "righteousness of the saints" is plural and cannot refer to the imparted righteousness of Christ, which is the believer's portion, but the righteousnesses which have survived examination and have become the basis of reward. (3) In 1 Corinthians 4:5; 2 Timothy 4:8; and Revelation 22:12 the

reward is associated with "that day," that is, the day in which He comes for His own. Thus it must be observed that the rewarding of the church must take place between the rapture and the revelation of Christ to the earth.[4]

Figure 4
The *Bema* in Relation to the Rapture and the Tribulation

	Bema		White Throne	
	Rapture	2d Advent	Judgment	
THE CHURCH AGE	TRIBULATION	MILLENNIUM	ETERNAL STATE
Present	7 Years	1000 Years	
		Messianic Kingdom	

This then is the object of New Testament prophecy —preparing the believer to be ready to stand in the presence of Jesus. Because the rapture can take place at any moment, the *bema* is also imminent. We have no guarantee that we will see tomorrow before our Lord returns for us—when we must give an account of our lives to Him. Thus, the *bema* may be close at hand.

Notes

1. The term *Millennium* is actually a Latin word meaning one thousand, because Revelation 20 says that Satan will be bound for one thousand years while Jesus rules Israel and the rest of the world from the throne of King David. From this term have developed the titles for the three major approaches to biblical prophecy:

    (1) the *premillennial* view, which teaches that Jesus will return before the Millennium (this view applies a normal, or literal, principle of interpretation when interpreting biblical prophecy);

    (2) the *postmillennial* view, which teaches that Christian influence will spread worldwide and the church will exercise dominion for many centuries before Jesus returns for a general judgment and the introduction of the eternal state (this view applies a nonliteral, allegorical, or spiritual principle of interpretation when interpreting prophecy and references to Israel);

    (3) the *amillennial* view, which teaches that Jesus is coming back to carry out a general judgment and introduce the eternal state, but that there will be no literal millennial rule either by the church or by Jesus (this view also applies an allegorical or spiritual principle of interpretation).

    This book assumes the premillennial approach, since it uses the same principle of interpretation when interpreting prophecy as all evangelicals use when interpreting other portions of Scripture.

2. The Scriptures indicate that the messiah will be revealed in some way three different times before the second advent. The exact order is not clearly stated but may be deduced:

(1) the revelation to the church at the rapture (1 Thessalonians 4:13-18);

(2) the revelation to the Gentile nations when the unbelieving cry out in fear of the one who sits on the throne (Revelation 6:12-17); and

(3) the revelation to Israel when the 144,000 Israelis are converted and sealed (Zechariah 12:10; Revelation 6:12-17).

3. There are three major views concerning the time of the rapture that are held by premillennialists:

(1) the *pretribulation rapture* view, which holds that the rapture will precede the Tribulation period;

(2) the *midtribulation rapture* view, which holds that the rapture will take place in the middle of the seven-year Tribulation period;

(3) the *posttribulation rapture* view, which holds that the rapture will take place at the end of the Tribulation period, at the same time that the second advent occurs.

It appears to me that there is a great deal of evidence in the Scriptures pointing to the pretribulation rapture view. However, the point of Scripture is not that the Christian will not have to suffer tribulation or persecution, for Paul says that all who live godly lives will suffer persecution of some kind. Rather, the emphasis of scriptural references to the rapture seems to be on the fact that we can be surprised by the rapture at anytime, and thus our lives should be affected by that truth.

4. J. Dwight Pentecost, *Things to Come* (Findlay, Ohio: Dunham, 1958), pp. 220-21.

7

Signs of an Imminent *Bema*

The world is changing, and in many cases, radically. Some of these changes appear to be significant prophetically.[1] Scripture reveals a number of the characteristics of world affairs that will occur prior to or during the Tribulation period. Following are a few of them, along with what appear to be some current preparatory signs. Each of those signs is a reminder that not only is the Tribulation period coming but with it will also come the rapture of the church and the *bema*.

THE SIGNS

SIGNIFICANT MILITARY ACTIVITY IN THE MIDDLE EAST

In the last days many nations will focus great amounts of military might on the Middle Eastern countries, leading up to the final military campaign called the "Battle of Jehoshaphat" in Joel 3:1-2 and the "Battle of Armageddon" in Revelation 16:16. Daniel 11 describes much of the detail of this final war that is climaxed by the coming of the Lord of resurrection.

Sign: For the past four decades war has broken out repeatedly in the Middle East. The Arab-Israeli hatred and violence seems to be without relief. Also, with the rise of Islamic fundamentalism and nationalism and the perpetuation of the Palestinian problem, there has been an increase in resentment toward and terrorism against the West.

Sign: Through the wealth produced by massive petroleum resources, a number of the Middle Eastern Arab nations have become extremely powerful militarily, while at the same time most of the industrial nations have become greatly dependent on Middle Eastern oil. The Iraqi invasion of Kuwait and the swift and decisive military response by the United States and other nations underscores the strong possibility of a major conflagration in the region in the future.

A UNITED EUROPE

The countries that make up what used to be the Roman Empire must come together in the last days, and the Antichrist must rule over a united Europe (Daniel 2 and 9).

Sign: November 1989—For days television, radio, and newspapers continually reported on the most significant international event in the decade. The Berlin Wall, symbol of the Cold War and the failure of Communism, was crumbling. Europe was changing—and radically. Most of the nations of eastern Europe were moving toward greater democratization and openness to the West. In 1990 the two Germanies were reunited.

Sign: 1989-1992—The European Community forges ahead with the removal of trade barriers between nations, the election of a European Parliament, and a commitment to a common currency. Tunnels and bridges are under construction that will link England with France, and Germany and Denmark with Sweden and Norway. Some foresee a united Europe that could become the strongest economic force in the world.

INTERNATIONAL ECONOMICS

During the Tribulation period the Antichrist will institute an international economic system involving some kind of mark on the hand or forehead as a requirement for being able to buy and sell in the marketplace (Revelation 13; 17; 18).

Sign: October 1987—The U.S. stock market crashed, with resounding ripples felt around the world from London to Tokyo to Hong Kong, evidence that the world economic system was becoming increasingly interdependent.

Sign: Computer driven bar-code systems are now common. This technology could utilize marks on a person's hand or forehead to force him to bend to the will of the person or persons who control the world's economies.

WAR AND PEACE

In the last days, prior to Christ's return, there will be wars and rumors of wars, but right before the terrible wrath of the Day of the Lord, people will be obsessed with peace and safety (Matthew 24: 1 Thessalonians 5).

Sign: There have been more wars in the twentieth century than in any other century in the history of mankind, yet talk of peace dominates the news in both the East and the West. In 1988 Russia and major portions of eastern Europe, under the leadership and influence of Mikhail Gorbachev, began to make strides toward political reform, open borders, and disarmament. For a time U. S. President George Bush and the Russian leader seemed to be competing for the spotlight as peacebrokers.

ISRAEL AND THE TEMPLE

During the Tribulation period the Antichrist will invade Jerusalem, stop the sacrifices, and defile the Temple by proclaiming himself to be God and setting up an abominable idol ("the abomination of desolation") in the Holy Place in the Temple. Therefore, by that time Israel must be regathered to Palestine, have possession of Jerusalem, and control the Temple mount. She must rebuild her Temple and institute Temple sacrifices again (Daniel 9; 11; Amos 9; Zechariah 14; Matthew 24; 2 Thessalonians 2).

Sign: Israel became a nation in 1948.

Sign: Israel captured Jerusalem in 1967.

Sign: October 1989—*Time* magazine reported astounding progress in Israel toward rebuilding the Temple and the reestablishment of the sacrificial system. Two Talmudic schools in Jerusalem are teaching nearly two hundred students how to carry on temple services. Jews who believe they are of priestly descent plan a convention in Jerusalem in the near future. Former Chief Rabbi Shlomo Goren and his organization claim to have located the site of the ancient Holy of Holies. The Temple Institute is researching and constructing the more than one hundred different ritual implements for Temple sacrifices, and the Institute is preparing blueprints for a million dollar authentic replica of the Temple. A 1983 newspaper poll reported that up to 18.3 percent of Israelis thought it was time to rebuild the Temple.[2]

EARTHQUAKES

In His Olivet Discourse Jesus prophesied that the world would witness earthquakes in various places (Matthew 24:7).

Sign: October 1989—An earthquake of devastating proportions (over 7.0 on the Richter scale) rocked the California Bay Area. In the preceding two decades newspapers carried front page stories of numerous earthquakes worldwide, including earthquakes in the United States, Europe, Russian Armenia, Japan, and Central America.[3]

A WORLD DICTATOR

Out of what was once the Roman Empire a world dictator will arise, the Antichrist (Daniel 2; 7; 9).

Sign: As the two Germanies united in 1990, fear of antisemitism and the rise of a powerful demagogue out of central Europe grew. In the July 15, 1990, *Denver Post* an article on developments in eastern Europe written by Lars-Erik Nelson warned that "somewhere in this mix there could be great potential for a future demagogue: Someone who could rise to power by capitalizing on unemployment, rising prices, the resurgence of nationalism, anti-Semitism and nostalgia for what may one day seem like a golden socialist past."

A *BEMA* MENTALITY

What does all of this mean? I believe there is a definite message from God in these events: Christian, wake up! This may be your time to give an account to Jesus.

Although for the past two centuries books, pamphlets, and sermons on prophetic topics have proliferated, I fear that the primary purposes of prophecy often have been lost or diluted. Many regard prophecy as but an enjoyable intellectual pursuit or a means to satisfy one's curiosity about the future.

The Bible reveals a number of notable purposes for prophecy. Prophecy authenticates divine revelation. It stabilizes believers in the face of disturbing events. It provides comfort. And it motivates the believer to live life in purity and faithfulness to the Lord.

The latter is probably the most important. Prophecy is meant to draw our attention to the reality and the imminency of our Lord's return and our subsequent evaluation at the *bema*. As we see signs pointing to Jesus' coming, we should have a *bema* mentality, an expectant attitude that drives us to prepare to meet and be evaluated by Jesus imminently.

A *bema* mentality encourages and cheers the informed believer; it continually impels him to a life of faithfulness, purity, and godly tolerance; and it produces an overpowering ambition to please Jesus.

I once heard of a duck who somehow had broken his wing on his way south for the winter. A farmer picked him up and took him home. The children of the house petted and coddled him, feeding him from the table and taking him along as they did their daily chores. They were heartbroken that next fall as they watched him struggle to join the ducks who were flying south. His wing just wasn't that strong yet. Longingly, he looked up every time a flock flew over.

The second year his wing was much stronger. But the children had fed him so well that as he attempted to take off, he was too fat to get airborne. He tried once or twice, then failed and turned back to the children to play.

The third year as the other ducks quacked their call to go south, he never even looked up as they flew over.

When life is comfortable it is easy to disregard who we are and where we are destined to be. We fall into a fat-duck mentality, lazy and content, forgetting that the Lord wants us to live with a *bema* mentality, always watching and longing to "fly away" to meet Jesus.

Be alert: Keep your life pure!

Be sober: Make your life count!

Be expectant: Look forward to His coming!

And join with those who share the expectation expressed in H. L. Turner's *Christ Returneth!*

It may be at morn, when the day is awaking,
When sunlight thru darkness and shadow is breaking
That Jesus will come in the fullness of glory
To receive from the world His own.

It may be at midday, it may be at twilight,
It may be, perchance that the blackness of midnight
Will burst into light in the blaze of His glory,
When Jesus receives His own.

O joy! O delight! should we go without dying,
No sickness, no sadness, no dread and no crying,
Caught up thru the clouds with our Lord into glory,
When Jesus receives His own.

O Lord Jesus, how long, how long
Ere we shout the glad song:
Christ returneth! Hallelujah!
Hallelujah! Amen, Hallelujah! Amen.

Notes

1. These are but a few of the many worldwide developments that could well be signs of preparation for the events of the last days. Jesus also referred to the rise of false Christs, famines, persecution, pestilences, betrayal and hatred, false prophets, lawlessness, lovelessness, and worldwide evangelism as signs pointing to His soon return (Matthew 24:4-14).
2. "Time for a New Temple?" *Time,* October 16, 1989, pp. 64-65.
3. Although the number of earthquakes may not have actually increased in recent years, they seem to have been centered in large urban areas, causing considerable damage and loss of life. News coverage has been extensive. This increased "awareness" may have been what Jesus was referring to.

Part 2

HEAVENLY REWARDS
AND LOSS AND SHAME
AT THE *BEMA*

8

Our Eternal Rewards

I remember one of the first times I ran in a track meet in high school, I got a third place ribbon. It was in the 440—and I still remember the thrill of walking up to get that ribbon. There is something exciting and fulfilling about receiving an award at the climax of a challenge. Imagine what it will be like to stand in the presence of Jesus Christ to receive rewards from Him.

REWARDS IN THE BIBLE

A number of terms are used in the Greek New Testament to convey the idea of rewards. The primary word translated "reward" is *misthos* and its derivatives. In the New Testament it carries both the idea of payment for a job one is hired to do (e.g., Matthew 20:8) as well as honor for a job well done, possibly with some sacrifice (e.g., Luke 6:23).[1]

The Bible describes many different rewards and often reveals the specific life challenges for which each is intended. How figuratively some of those rewards are to be taken we cannot be certain—whether, for example, we actually get real crowns, or whether the crowns represent something even greater than crowns. In any case, Paul seems to indicate in 1 Corinthians 9:25 that whatever we receive, it will certainly be real and have eternal value.

Often we read biblical passages that refer to some heavenly reward and pass over the eternal significance of what is being said. To help direct our focus to the reality of those eternal rewards, I have attempted to summarize and categorize the various New Testament references to rewards.

TREASURE IN HEAVEN

Jesus Himself taught us about earthly and heavenly treasures: "Do not lay up for yourselves treasures upon earth where moth and rust destroy and where thieves break in and steal; but lay up for yourselves treasures in heaven where neither moth nor rust destroys and where thieves do not break in and steal" (Matthew 6:19-20). Similarly, Paul exhorts us to invest bountifully in heavenly treasure: "But this I say: He who sows sparingly will also reap sparingly, and he who sows bountifully will also reap bountifully" (2 Corinthians 9:6).

Jesus probably used the term *treasure* as a synonym for rewards in general. In the reference to treasure in Matthew 6 and in and many other instances, both the Lord and the apostles spoke of eternal rewards in the context of specific conditions God requires for rewards. In chapter 10 we will refer to many of those conditions as "insider information for investing in heavenly rewards." At this point we want simply to observe that the promise of heavenly treasure relates not only to that which is religious but to all of life. God is concerned about everything that we do.

INHERITANCE

A second way of describing heavenly rewards is in terms of our inheritance. Hebrews 6:12 exhorts us to move forward in our spiritual growth in order that we might participate in the inheritance planned for us, claiming the promises of that inheritance: "That you do not become sluggish, but imitate those who with faith and patience inherit the promises" (Hebrews 6:12).

All believers. Obviously, all believers are heirs (1 Peter 1:3-4).[2] But in the book of Hebrews it does seem that a distinction is made between those who participate in the blessings of the inheritance and those who do not. All believers will inherit an eternal home in heaven, glorified bodies, an eternal relationship with God that allows them to enter freely into the throne room of God. All believers enjoy the blessings of living forever in the new heavens and the new earth, and all believers inherit the blessings of being with their believing loved ones in eternity—all simply by their faith in Jesus Christ.

Participation in the blessings of the inheritance. But there seems to be more than this basic inheritance, as wonderful as it is. There is more to what God has promised to us. Those who persevere in faith, claiming the promises of God and maintaining their confidence in the reality of the coming inheritance, will enjoy the fullness of the inheritance.

In the Old Testament the people of Israel were heirs of wonderful promises given to their fathers, Abraham, Isaac, and Jacob. Theirs was the Promised Land, with many wonderful attendant blessings. However, the writer of Hebrews reminds us that there were people who missed the blessings of participating in that inheritance. Those people wandered in the desert for forty years, because when God offered them the promises they refused to believe God and backed off (Hebrews 3:7–4:13).

Later in the book of Hebrews (12:14-17) the author states that Esau missed the blessings of the inheritance because he was more materially minded than he was heavenly minded. It appears that full participation in the inheritance issue awaits those people who can see that there are greater things ahead, and that it is worthwhile to walk by faith now, to remain true to God, and to continue in a persevering trust in God.

Special inheritance for those who suffer with Christ. Paul wrote in Romans 8:16-17 of the possibility of being more than an heir of God. He declares that we can share in the inheritance of Christ as a co-heir: "The Spirit Himself bears witness with our spirit that we are children of God, and if children, then heirs—heirs of God and joint heirs with Christ, if indeed we suffer with Him, that we may also be glorified together."

Jesus is described as the "firstborn among many brethren" (Romans 8:29) and the "firstborn from the dead" (Colossians

1:18). The term *firstborn* was a legal term indicating the person who had primary right to the family inheritance. It was used of King David in Psalm 89:26 to indicate that he was appointed the ruling heir of the kingdom of Israel. In Paul's use of the term he may be telling us that if we are among those who suffer with Christ we may possibly have a special place of rule with Christ over the primary eternal inheritance.

If so, that would add light to Paul's statement about his heart's desire to experience the fellowship of Christ's suffering (Philippians 3:10), and it may be what Paul had in mind in his encouraging words in 2 Corinthians 4: "For our light affliction, which is but for a moment, is working for us a far more exceeding and eternal weight of glory" (v. 17).

Three other apostles alluded to a special inheritance or crown for enduring suffering for Christ's sake. James and John both wrote about the wreath-crown "of life," and both stated that the condition for receiving this crown was endurance through suffering for the Lord's sake (James 1:12; Revelation 2:10). In the midst of teaching how to respond to persecuting authority in the home, in business, and in civil affairs, Peter firmly exhorted believers not to return "evil for evil or reviling for reviling, but on the contrary blessing, knowing that you were called to this, that you may inherit a blessing" (1 Peter 3:9).

Put another way, Peter was saying that if we respond to evil and insults in the same way that Jesus responded to them we will inherit a special blessing in eternity. The context of 1 Peter provides a number of applications of this principle. A wife married to a man prone to abusive language may exercise this principle by not responding in kind. An employee who is repeatedly harassed by his boss for not compromising his convictions may exercise this principle by carefully avoiding any semblance of vengeance or hatred. A person who faces lawsuits and jail because he took a stand as a Christian for the rights of the unborn may exercise this principle by continuing to express love even for the judge and the news reporters covering the case. The family of a missionary who was rejected and killed by those to whom he has gone to share the love of God can exercise this principle by continuing to serve Christ and praying for the salvation of the murderers. Believers who so respond to evil will receive a special blessing in their inheritance and may possibly be among the co-heirs with Christ.

Special parts of our inheritance. In a few passages the New Testament describes specific parts of the inheritance to come and often mentions the conditions for receiving each part.

Jesus taught that the "meek" would inherit the earth, possibly referring to a special place of rule in the future for those who now do not demand their own rights (Matthew 5:5). The book of Hebrews maintains that those who demonstrate faith and patience now will "inherit the promises" (Hebrews 6:12). Peter teaches that those who are characterized by "not rendering evil for evil, or railing for railing; but blessing" will be able to "inherit a blessing" (1 Peter 3:9). A primary contribution to the believer's preparation for receiving eternal inheritances, Paul told the Ephesian elders, was the "word of His grace, which is able to build you up" (Acts 20:32), a reference, apparently, to the wonderful grace teaching of the New Testament.

Inherit the kingdom of God. A phrase concerning inheritance that appears in Paul's epistles is "inherit the kingdom of God": "Do you not know that the unrighteous will not inherit the kingdom of God? Do not be deceived. Neither fornicators, nor idolaters, nor adulterers, nor homosexuals, nor sodomites, nor thieves, nor covetous, nor drunkards, nor revilers, nor extortioners will inherit the kingdom of God" (1 Corinthians 6:9-10). A similar statement is found in Galatians 5:21. Some interpret the passage as a general description of an unbeliever, indicating a lifestyle as opposed to committing a particular act. This view asserts that a true born-again Christian would never fall into the habit of doing any of these sins. However, Paul most likely is using the phrase "inherit the kingdom" in terms of being a part of those who have a share in the rule of the eternal kingdom. He is not saying that the one described will be eliminated from living eternally in heaven but that he will come up empty-handed in the messianic kingdom.

REST

In the book of Hebrews, with the Old Testament example of Israel in the wilderness in the background, a major part of our inheritance is described as "rest." Rest does not refer to sitting around doing nothing or sleeping in the kingdom. It refers to what the children of Israel did not have while they were under God's discipline and outside the Promised Land, not enjoying their inheritance. (For the opposite of rest, see Deuteronomy 28:64-67.) The word *rest* is therefore a way of describing the full enjoyment of the inheritance of God. The full inheritance is enjoyed by those who now walk by faith and not by sight.

RULE/DOMINION

The fourth type of reward is described in Luke 19. In the parable of the minas a remarkable statement about rewards is given (a mina was equivalent to about $5,000 in today's economy):

> Now as they heard these things, He spoke another parable, because He was near Jerusalem and because they thought the kingdom of God would appear immediately.
> Therefore He said, "A certain nobleman went into a far country to receive for himself a kingdom and to return. So he called ten of his servants, delivered to them ten minas, and said to them, 'Do business till I come.'" (Luke 19:11-13)

When the nobleman returned from his trip he called the slaves together for an accounting.

> The first appeared saying, "Master, your $5000 has made ten times more. You now have $55,000."
> So the Master said to him, "You did a good job, slave. Since you have been faithful in a very little thing, I will give you authority to rule over ten cities." (Luke 19:16-17 [paraphrased])

Now, whatever else is involved in this parable, it does appear that Jesus is saying that the believer's faithful service and carrying out of the stewardship with which he has been charged is connected to the kind of authority he will be given in the messianic kingdom.

The history of the planet and God's program for the conflict of the ages centers around God's purpose of reestablishing man's dominion under God's authority. Ultimately, at the end of this age, when He establishes His messianic kingdom under the second Adam (the last Adam), Jesus Christ, the King of kings and Lord of lords, man will once again be established in his intended position. When Christ was raised from the dead, He was given this authority as the chosen, perfect man (Matthew 28:18; Romans 1:4).

And we will join with Christ in this blessed rule. Mankind will be back in the position for which God had originally intended him—ruling over the entire universe.

What are we are going to rule over? Each other? No, for all of us are royal priests (Revelation 1:6). All of us will have some kind of rule. But we are told that the entire universe is inhabited by angels. Some of these inhabitants are called cherubs; others are called seraphs. Still others can be found at varying levels of divinely given authority. We are told in 1 Corinthians that we will judge angels (1 Corinthians 6:3). Judging seems to imply some kind of rule. So the church is designed to rule over creatures throughout the universe.

Our coming rule will begin with the Millennium, so we will not only judge angels but will rule people living on the earth between the time of the second advent of Christ and the end of Millennium. During that period of time there will be living nations and, because we reign with Him, rule over them must be a part of our charge as well.

It may be inferred that there will be a particular place on this or another planet where each of us will be appointed to rule—and the extent of that rule will be determined by our wise stewardship in this life.

DIVINE COMMENDATION

In His prophetic sermon, the Olivet Discourse, Jesus specified another important reward: public commendation by the

Master: "Well done, good and faithful servant; you were faithful over a few things, I will make you ruler over many things. Enter into the joy of your Lord" (Matthew 25:21).

"Well done, good and faithful servant"—what a marvelous commendation from our Lord.

In the spring of 1990 the Fellowship of Christian Athletes gave the Man of the Year award for a second time to University of Colorado football coach Bill McCartney. Providing the introduction to the award was Senator Bill Armstrong of Colorado. Armstrong made a spiritually incisive statement about McCartney's acclaim. Armstrong said that now were the crowds, the cheers, the cheerleaders, and the applause, but the only thing that really counts will be the commendation of Jesus Christ for McCartney's bold testimony and service to Him, when Jesus will welcome His servant home with the words "Well done, good and faithful servant."

In addition to Jesus' *commendation,* He is also prepared to *confess us publicly* before the angels: "Also I say to you, whoever confesses Me before men, him the Son of Man also will confess before the angels of God" (Luke 12:8).

A ROYAL WELCOME

In the introduction to his second epistle, Peter describes a mature Christian. In that description he introduces another special reward, a royal welcome:

> Therefore, brethren, be all the more diligent to make certain about his calling and choosing you. For as long as you practice these things you will never stumble. For in this way, the *entrance into the eternal kingdom* of our lord and Savior, Jesus Christ, will be *abundantly supplied* to you. (2 Peter 1:11, italics added)

The word here for "entrance" is the Greek word *eisodos.* The term literally means "the way in." In Greece today a door might be labeled *eisodos,* "entrance," or *exodos,* "exit." As an extension of this basic meaning *eisodos* can also mean "reception," or "welcome." It is this latter meaning that Peter certainly had in mind.

Another instructive term used in the passage is the word *abundant,* a translation of a form of the Greek word for wealth. The Greek term can also be translated "richly," or "in full measure." Peter is saying that at our entrance into the eternal messianic kingdom our Lord and Savior will richly and abundantly welcome us.

That sounds to me like the red carpet treatment. There might even be rows of angels there to welcome us as Jesus puts His arm around us and publicly confesses, "Here is one of My disciples who grew in spiritual graces and served Me well!"

SPECIAL TREATMENT BY THE MASTER

Another special reward described in Scripture is mentioned in Luke. This reward is quite remarkable. "Blessed are those servants whom the master, when he comes, will find watching. Assuredly, I say to you that he will gird himself and have them sit down to eat, and will come and serve them" (12:37).

Jesus implies that at His coming He will wait on His "watching" servant. I don't know exactly what Peter felt like when Jesus washed his feet. But I am sure that after the embarrassment was over, there was a rich feeling of favor and love.

Even in His royalty and deity, Jesus will reward some of us with a special, personal ministry he will carry out Himself.

REJOICING

First Peter 4:12-13 and Matthew 25:21 indicate that there is a special experience of joy in the presence of the Lord for those who have suffered with Him, and for those who have been faithful stewards.

THE OVERCOMER REWARDS

There is another list of rewards in Revelation 1-3. To each of the seven churches addressed Jesus promises special re-

wards for overcomers. The passages in Revelation are somewhat debatable, however. Depending on how you define the
term *overcomer* one can either say that the rewards in view are
ones all believers will receive or that they are rewards only a
special group of overcoming Christians will receive. Whoever is
to receive them, it is evident that they are precious, prized
rewards.

1. Special access to the tree of life (2:7)
2. Protection from any ill effects when the unbeliever is
   judged at the great white throne and punished with the
   second death (2:10-11)
3. Provision of the hidden manna and the white stone
   with a new name known only to the recipient (2:17)
4. The morning star (2:28)
5. Being clothed in white garments and confessed before
   the heavenly father and the holy angels (3:5)
6. Becoming a pillar in the Temple of God and being labeled with God's name, the name of the New Jerusalem, and Jesus' new name (3:12).
7. Being allowed to sit with Christ on His throne (3:21)

WREATH-CROWNS

The wreath-crowns are the most prominent of the rewards
mentioned in the New Testament. In the last section of this
book those special rewards will be discussed.

BE A WINNER

We need to look on life from the standpoint of a race that
we want to win. To win the "race of life" does not necessarily
mean that we are great or that we accomplish great things in
the way history might evaluate it. To be a winner in God's sight
is to complete the course God has designed for us. It is to be
faithful to Him all the way to the end, to persevere.

Trust God and claim His promise to do great things in
your life.

Be a faithful servant of Jesus Christ!

Be a winner!

Go for the Gold!

Notes

1. Other related terms are *antapodoma, antapodosis, apodidomi, misthapodotes* and *komizo*.

2. Ephesians 1 also speaks of inheritance as it relates to all believers, but most likely Paul's thought here is that believers are saints who are *God's* inheritance and a means of bringing glory to God.

9
Divine Principles
for Rewarding Saints

Psalm 90, "a Prayer of Moses the man of God," contains these
words:

> For all our days have passed away in Your wrath;
> We finish our years like a sigh.
> The days of our lives are seventy years;
> And if by reason of strength they are eighty years,
> Yet their boast is only labor and sorrow;
> For it is soon cut off, and we fly away.
> Who knows the power of Your anger?
> For as the fear of You, so is Your wrath.
> So teach us to number our days,
> That we may gain a heart of wisdom.
>
> (Psalm 90:9-12)

Our lives are short when compared to the recorded history of
mankind and but a whisper in the night compared to the end-
less reaches of eternity. How we use our few short days is extremely significant.

Often as people reach midlife they take stock as to what
has truly been worthwhile in their lives. How they wished they
had thought more seriously about their career choices and time

commitments. But how much more sobering is the thought that there will be a time when we will all look back over our entire lives—in the presence of Christ—and take final stock. It makes each moment of each day and all of our decisions and priorities seem far more important than we normally take them.

But often we are not quite sure how to set our priorities. Understanding the principles Jesus will employ at the *bema* will furnish a framework for deciding what is truly important and will help us to set right priorities and live worthwhile lives. Those principles can significantly affect all of our decisions and time priorities. I call them "the divine principles for rewarding saints."[1]

Before proceeding with this discussion, it should be recognized that some of the principles come from passages that describe Jesus' plans for judging groups of believers other than those that make up the church specifically (i.e., Old Testament and Tribulation saints). It seems reasonable to me, however, to conclude that the same principles apply to us, since we are all the people of God and all have the same judge, Jesus Christ, who is appointed by the Father to carry out all judgment (John 5:22).[2]

TWELVE PRINCIPLES OF DIVINE REWARD

Principle #1: Jesus will judge our deeds, our words, our thoughts, and our motives.

Our deeds. In a general statement in Romans, Paul declares that God's judgment will take into account our deeds: "God... 'will render to each one according to his deeds'" (Romans 2:5b-6). Then in a specific reference to the *bema* in 2 Corinthians 5:10, he says, "For we must all appear before the judgment seat of Christ, that each one may receive the things done in the body, according to what he has done, whether good or bad" (2 Corinthians 5:10).

Our words. In his epistle James bluntly warns us of the difficulty of taming the tongue. Teachers—whose vocation is words—are warned that they will receive a stricter judgment

(James 3). Jesus taught that "for every idle word men may speak, they will give account of it in the day of judgment. For by your words you will be justified, and by your words you will be condemned" (Matthew 12:36-37).

Our thoughts and motives. Behind every word and every deed are the thoughts and motives of the unseen world of our minds. To Jesus this region is like a transparent bowl: everything is visible. At the *bema* our thoughts and our motives will be made completely manifest.

From what Paul says in 1 Corinthians 3 and 4, it would seem that the motive ultimately will be the deciding factor of that which is gold, silver, and precious stones. And Jesus said, "For there is nothing covered that will not be revealed, nor hidden that will not be known" (Luke 12:3). The book of Hebrews reinforces this statement: "For the word of God is living and powerful, and sharper than any two-edged sword, piercing even to the division of soul and spirit, and of joints and marrow, and is a discerner of the thoughts and intents of the heart. And there is no creature hidden from His sight, but all things are naked and open to the eyes of Him to whom we must give account" (Hebrews 4:12-13).

Right after Paul describes the process of the *bema* judgment in 1 Corinthians 3, he addresses the principle of judgment of thoughts and motives:

> Moreover it is required in stewards that one be found faithful. But with me it is a very small thing that I should be judged by you or by a human court. In fact, I do not even judge myself. For I know nothing against myself, yet I am not justified by this; but He who judges me is the Lord. Therefore judge nothing before the time until the Lord comes, who will both bring to light the hidden things of darkness and reveal the counsels of the hearts; and then each one's praise will come from God. (1 Corinthians 4:2-5)

In other words, don't spend hours and hours in self-examination to the point that you become introspective. Don't spend your time looking at how well or how poorly others are performing, either, but wait until the Lord comes. He will bring to light what is hidden now and disclose the true motives behind our public actions. Then each man will be rewarded (praised) by the Lord.

Yes, He will reveal our thoughts and everything that is hidden—the things no one else knows about. Our personal loving relationship with God and our quiet times alone with the Lord will be revealed—but our lustful desires and hateful thoughts will also be brought to light.

Our thoughts and our true motives will be displayed at the *bema*. Paul speaks of the "counsels of our hearts," referring to the decisions or purposes that are in the deepest part of the soul. The book of Hebrews says that not only the thoughts but the intents of the heart are opened by the Lord's word (4:12; the Greek term carries the idea of thoughts deep in the mind, of deliberations, insights, and perceptions).

The issue of motive raises two major questions and problems regarding practical application: Should I do something if I don't feel like it? Is not working for rewards under any circumstance prompted by unworthy and selfish motives?

What about doing something even if I don't feel like it? When I was a pastor and asked an individual to do a particular job in the church, sometimes I would receive the reply, "I don't want to teach that Sunday school class because I don't feel like it—and since I don't feel like it, my motive would be wrong if I took the job. So I can't help you."

Or I would ask someone, "Can you help out in the nursery?" Sometimes the reply would be, "That is really not my gift. I don't like doing it that much, so if I did it, it would be in the flesh—and I want to do things that I am motivated to do in such a fashion that it is in the spirit and I feel really good about it. Why don't you ask someone else to help?"

Those responses are not what motive is all about. Having a good motive doesn't mean doing only the things we like to do and not doing the things we don't want to do.

Can you imagine telling the mother who changes the dirty diapers of her child—something she surely doesn't like to do very much—that she has the wrong motive for doing it?

Can you imagine saying that when Jesus went to the cross —something He obviously did not "enjoy" doing—He had the wrong motive? To the contrary: the things we do not feel the most like doing but which we do because of love and faithfulness are usually the ones that are done with the best of motives.

What about working for rewards being an unworthy and selfish motive? An answer to this question requires an analysis of kinds of motives revealed in Scripture. The Scriptures condemn certain motives as sinful. James declares that envy of others and the desire to push oneself ahead of others are both evil (James 3:14-16). Obviously any action that is produced by greed, hatred, immoral desires, or anger is also evil (Ephesians 4:17–5:5). On the other hand, actions produced by the attitudes of love, faithfulness, and thankfulness are good ones (Romans 12:9-11; Galatians 5:22,23; and 1 Thessalonians 5:18).

But there is another motive that is often overlooked—the motive of faith, faith in the promises of God. Hebrews makes it clear that persevering faith will be rewarded: "But without faith it is impossible to please Him, for he who comes to God must believe that He is, and that He is a rewarder of those who diligently seek Him" (Hebrews 11:6). It is possible for a person to have selfish and mixed motives at best and still receive rewards, simply because he really believes that God will reward him. Such was the case of conniving Jacob. He cheated his brother Esau out of his birthright to the rewards of the divine inheritance. Nevertheless, he received great reward as the progenitor of the nation of Israel and future blessings in the messianic kingdom, because he acted out of faith.

A person who serves God simply because he truly believes that God will reward him for his service may lack many of the higher motives for his actions and thus miss much of his reward, but it is certain that he *will* receive reward.

When I was a child, I often did jobs around the house in my father's absence just because I loved him and looked forward to the reward of his good pleasure on his return. Love and looking forward to rewards are certainly not mutually exclusive.

Serving God for rewards alone is not a sinful motive but is instead a valid and important one. Service for rewards alone will be greatly enriched if it is accompanied by other motives, too, such as love and thanksgiving.

Principle #2: Only what Christ through the Holy Spirit produces in our lives has any value at the *bema.*

Christ said, "I am the vine. You are the branches. He who abides in Me and I in him, bears much fruit, for without me, you can do nothing" (John 15:5). If this verse is to be read literally and absolutely, we must conclude that unless Jesus Christ is producing something of value in us, our efforts are absolutely worthless. One old preacher put it this way: "Nothing means nothing—like a zero with the rim knocked off."

Paul says the same thing: "I have been crucified with Christ; it is no longer I who live, but Christ lives in me; and the life which I now live in the flesh I live by faith in the Son of God, who loved me and gave Himself for me" (Galatians 2:20). Our lives have value only as a product of our faith in Jesus Christ. Christ will value only those deeds done in the context of our abiding relationship with Him—those done as we walk in the Spirit.

Principle #3: Jesus will reward us according to our persevering faith in God and His promises.

The book of Hebrews teaches much about rewards, describing them in terms of the promise of rest (3:7-4:11), the inheritance of the promises (6:12, 15), receiving the promise (11:8, 40), inheriting the blessing (11:9; 12:17), a prepared city (11:16), and the joy set before Christ and us (12:2). In this context the book's theme unfolds and examples are given. Those who are heavenly minded and persevere in their faith will be greatly rewarded.

Abraham had persevering faith that looked for a heavenly country and a prepared city that he did not experience in this life. Likewise, Moses rejected Egypt and accepted the reproach of Christ because he had faith in the future reward promised by the "invisible" God. But Esau, the brother of Jacob, missed his inheritance. He gave up his birthright, and although he wanted to repent and get his birthright back, he had missed his opportunity to take seriously the promise of eternal rewards. Rewards in heaven awaited persevering Abraham and Moses, but an empty future awaited materialistic Esau.

Hebrews 6:12 states, "Do not become sluggish, but imitate those who through faith and patience [perseverance] inherit the promises." If you are going to receive the inheritance of God, hang in there—stick with the Lord and His promises. Hebrews 10:35-36 expresses this truth in different terms: "Therefore do not cast away your confidence, which has great reward. For you have need of endurance, so that after you have done the will of God, you may receive the promise."

Hebrews 11 is another passage that describes the kind of life that wins the reward. The chapter is filled with examples of people with living testimonies of the faithfulness of God and their trust in Him and His promises. Some of those people were killed; some suffered unimaginably. But all continued to believe in the future inheritance. As they continued to trust, they received repeated testimony from God as He answered prayer. Their testimonies are vivid reminders that persevering faith is necessary to fully participate in the inheritance promised to the people of God.

Principle #4: Jesus will reward us in proportion to our faithful and wise stewardship

In two masterful parables our Lord taught some important lessons about the relationship between stewardship and rewards.[3]

The parable of the talents. The parable of the talents appears in the Olivet Discourse, a prophetic message of Jesus recorded in Matthew 25:14-30. If Jesus were telling the same story today, it would probably sound something like this:

A man left on a long trip and entrusted his managers with thousands of dollars.[4] One manager was given $2 million; the second, $800,000; and the third, $400,000, each in accordance with his ability to manage. The first manager wisely invested his money in a diversified portfolio, and in a short time he had doubled his capital: $4 million. The second manager, likewise, exhibited his business acumen. He improved his stewardship allotment to more than $1.5 million. The third, however, put his $400,000 into a safe deposit box at the local bank, fearing the possibility of failure and his boss's anger.

After a long time, when the boss returned, he was pleased with the wise and faithful stewardship of the first two managers. In response, he praised them, delegated great authority to them commensurate with their performance, and invited them to participate with him in the joys of the leadership of the organization.

The lazy, unfaithful, unwise manager, who had no increase in his investment, was rebuked. His $400,000 was turned over to the first manager, and he was fired and restricted from company property. He went home with tears streaming down his face, gritting his teeth over how great an opportunity he had missed because of foolish, faithless fears.

The parable of the minas. A second, major stewardship parable our Lord taught is found in Luke 19:11-27. This story differs somewhat from the talents parable. The master is a nobleman, rather than just a man, and there are ten servants, not three. Each of the servants receives the same amount to invest. Only three of the servants are mentioned, and one has made a tenfold increase in his capital. In addition, the rule given to the wise servants is made specific in terms of rule over cities. Otherwise the parables are similar.

Conclusions to be drawn from the two parables. Both parables contain similar messages concerning the relationship of stewardship to subsequent rewards and position in eternity. Obviously, Jesus is represented by both the wealthy man and the nobleman. Each leaves for a time, picturing Jesus' absence between his first and second comings. The talents and minas symbolize all that Jesus has given us to be used wisely in His absence: our physical capabilities, our natural talents, our spiritual gifts, our training, our family ties, our wealth, our time, and our energy. In the mina parable, the citizens evidently represent the unbelieving Jews.

One can easily draw from the two stories important principles that apply to Jesus' judgment in the future and to our stewardship as Christians:

1. According to the talent parable, not all of us are given the same gifts from God. So He holds us responsible, not for what we do not have, but for what we do have to invest. Some people can sing, others have a superior intellect, and still others are gifted in leadership. Some can make money easily; others are sensitive and easily show mercy to those in need. Whatever God has given to us is what He demands we use for Him—and use wisely and faithfully.

2. The mina parable indicates that rewards and future responsibilities are not determined by how big a ministry we have but by how well we have used what God has given us and how large a percentage of return He gets on our investment.

3. Both parables teach that our stewardship now will affect the kind of responsibilities, honor, and authority we will have in the messianic kingdom.

4. Four traits of rewardable stewardship are mentioned:
   Goodness: Has the steward acted kindly and ethically?
   Faithfulness: Has the steward been loyal and responded to the master's desires?
   Wisdom: Has the steward chosen investment opportunities that produce the greatest amount of fruit of eternal value?
   Industry: Has the steward been lazy or hard at work in things that matter?

A friend of mine told me of a time when his entire business was destroyed in a flood on the Platte River in Denver. That night he went home to his wife, totally exhausted, and seemingly left with nothing. "You know, Honey," he said, "the only thing we have left is what we have given away." He understood what a wise investment is.

Principle #5: At the *bema* Jesus will take into account how we responded to the Word of God

Psalm 19 states that in the keeping of the law of the Lord is "great reward." God wants responsive people—people who study and apply the principles found in the Word of God. The man who would receive a reward does not necessarily have to be a scholar, but he must be one who "keeps" the law, not as one who arbitrarily discusses inanities but as one who makes a solid attempt to apply God's teaching to his own life.

Principle #6: At the *bema*, Jesus will be concerned with the purity of our lives

Paul was anxious that he not become morally disqualified in his intense race toward the end of his life and the judgment seat of Christ (1 Corinthians 9:27), and he also exhorted young Timothy to be diligent to present himself to the Lord as a workman who does not need to be ashamed (2 Timothy 2:15-23). The apostle John specifically warned believers to keep their lives pure, lest they face Jesus with shame at His coming (1 John 2:27–3:3).

When our Lord evaluates our lives, he will certainly be concerned about sin, because He expects His people to walk in holiness and purity of life and to grow to become more and more like Him.

I have a close friend who was an outstanding preacher and church planter. He was an effective teacher and a committed father. Then repeatedly he was unfaithful to his wife. From there he got into drugs to handle his guilt, then thievery to support his habit. As he was slipping further and further into this morass, I had the opportunity to visit with him. He told me he felt as though he still could hold onto one thing: that when he stood before the judgment seat of Christ the Lord would remember all the good things he had done—the people he had discipled and the churches he had started.

My response startled him. I told him that the New Testament implies that persevering "to the end" with purity and holy character may be necessary to receive most, if not all, the rewards mentioned in Scripture.

I am convinced that Jesus looks very carefully not only at what the vessel accomplishes but what kind of vessel it is. It will make a difference if the vessel has proved to be an impure one.

Principle #7: At the *bema* Jesus will take into account how long we have been saved

Matthew 20:1-16* is good news for those who become a child of God late in life.

> For the kingdom of heaven is like a landowner who went out early in the morning to hire laborers for his vineyard. Now when he had agreed with the laborers for a denarius a day, he sent them into his vineyard.
>
> And he went out about the third hour and saw others standing idle in the market place, and said to them, "You also go into the vineyard, and whatever is right I will give you." And they went.
>
> Again he went out about the sixth hour and the ninth hour, and did likewise. And about the eleventh hour he went out and found others standing idle, and said to them, "Why have you been standing here idle all day?"
>
> They said to him, "Because no one hired us."
>
> He said to them, "You also go into the vineyard, and whatever is right you will receive."
>
> So when evening had come, the owner of the vineyard said to his steward, "Call the laborers and give them their wages, beginning with the last to the first."

*Paragraph indentations follow the *New International Version.*

And when those came who were hired about the eleventh hour, they each received a denarius. But when the first came, they supposed that they would receive more; and they likewise received each a denarius. And when they had received it, they murmured against the landowner, saying, "These last men have worked only one hour, and you made them equal to us who have borne the burden and the heat of the day."

But he answered one of them and said, "Friend, I am doing you no wrong. Did you not agree with me for a denarius? Take what is yours and go your way. I wish to give to this last man the same as to you. Is it not lawful for me to do what I wish with my own things? Or is your eye evil because I am good?"

So the last will be first, and the first last. For many are called, but few chosen.

Jesus appears to be teaching that those who enter his service late in life may still receive significant rewards. He will not limit the rewards for those who have had little opportunity to serve.

Principle #8: Jesus will reward us according to our secondary involvement in the ministry of others

In Matthew 10:40-42 Jesus says, "He who receives you receives Me, and he who receives Me receives Him who sent Me. He who receives a prophet in the name of a prophet shall *receive a prophet's reward.* And he who receives a righteous man in the name of a righteous man shall *receive a righteous man's reward*"(italics added). This statement implies that those of us who support missionaries will receive the reward that the missionary receives for his service as well. If you house others who minister, such as missionaries; if you give them money, encourage them, visit their ministry to strengthen their morale, you share in their ministry. When that missionary receives his reward, I believe that Scripture teaches that you will stand with him and will participate in his reward.

Jesus doesn't say that you will get a *part* of his reward. He says you will get *his* reward. As a Christian looks forward to participating in the reward ceremony at the *bema,* he should aggressively support others who minister for the King.

Principle #9: If we judge others, Jesus will apply our standards when He judges us

Jesus states this sobering principle in the Sermon on the Mount: "Judge not, that you be not judged. For with what judgment you judge, you will be judged; and with the same measure you use, it will be measured back to you" (Matthew 7:1-2). The Bible is not clear as to exactly how, but somehow, some way, the gauge which we use to evaluate others on earth will be used to judge us in heaven.

On the other hand, if we show mercy, then mercy will be shown to us also. "For judgment is without mercy to the one who has shown no mercy. Mercy triumphs over judgment" (James 2:13); "Blessed are the merciful, for they shall obtain mercy" (Matthew 5:7).

Principle #10. Jesus will reward us for the results of our ministry in the lives of others

Referring to one kind of crown awarded at the *bema,* Paul identifies his ministry in the lives of the Thessalonians with his rewards: "For what is our hope, or joy, or crown of rejoicing? Is it not even you in the presence of our Lord Jesus Christ at His coming?" (1 Thessalonians 2:19).

In the context, Paul is talking about the converts he will present to Christ. Bringing people to Christ obviously pleases Him greatly.

Principle #11. Teachers will receive the stricter judgment

James, an apostle and a teacher, gives us this warning: "My brethren, let not many of you become teachers, knowing that we shall receive a stricter judgment" (James 3:1).

Principle #12. Not only production but contribution to production will receive reward

Our tendency is to focus our attention on the one who has the ministry that shows publicly—the preacher, the evangelistic harvester, the public leader. But the Scriptures say that different people have different gifts and contributions, and that all partake of rewards who contribute to the building of the Body of Christ. Paul says, "I planted, Apollos watered, but God gave the increase. So then neither he who plants is anything, nor he who waters, but God who gives the increase. Now he who plants and he who waters are one, and each one will receive his own reward according to his own labor" (1 Corinthians 3:6-8).

MAKE YOUR LIFE COUNT

Upon hearing of the assassination of John and Betty Stamm in China in 1934, Will Houghton, former president of Moody Bible Institute, penned these words:

> So this is life. This world with its pleasures, struggles, and tears, a smile, a frown, a sigh, friendship so true and love of kin and neighbor? Sometimes it is hard to live—always to die! The world moves on so rapidly for the living; the forms of those who disappear are replaced, and each one dreams that he will be enduring. How soon that one becomes the missing face! Help me to know the value of these hours. Help me the folly of all waste to see. Help me to trust the Christ who bore my sorrows and thus to yield for life or death to Thee.

Make your life count while your time lasts. Make your life count for eternity.

Notes

1. These principles are taken from both specifically defined *bema* passages and general passages on the interadvent period, as well as passages dealing with judgment in general.

2. The question as to when Old Testament and Tribulation saints will be evaluated by Jesus is not specifically addressed in Scripture. Most likely it will take place when their respective resurrections occur.

3. Another parable about a steward is found in Luke 16:1-13. Here, through the actions of an unjust steward, Jesus emphasizes again the importance of being faithful in wisely using the resources we have at our disposal.

4. A talent could be either gold or silver. A gold talent was worth more than $5 million, and a silver one about $400,000.

10

Insider Tips for Investing in Heavenly Treasure

Some time ago a friend of mine handed me a tongue-in-cheek investment opportunity letter he had just received.

Dear Art:

I don't know if you would be interested in the following, but I thought I would mention it to you because it could be a real "Sleeper" as regards making a LOT OF MONEY WITH VERY LITTLE INVESTMENT.

A group of us are considering investing in a large Cat Farm near Bogota, Columbia, in South America. It is our desire to start rather small with about one million cats. Each cat averages about twelve kittens each year; skins can be sold for about $.20 for the white ones and up to $.40 for the black ones. This will give us twelve million cat skins per year to sell at an average price of around $.32, giving us annual revenues of approximately $3,000,000 a year. This averages out to a gross profit of $10,000 a day, excluding Sundays and holidays.

In Bogota, a good cat skinner can skin about 50 cats per day at a wage of only $3.15 per day. It will only take 663 men to operate the ranch, so the net profit would be over $8,200 per day.

The cats would be fed on rats exclusively. Rats multiply four times as fast as cats. We anticipate starting a Rat Ranch adjacent to our Cat Farm. If we start with a million rats, we will have four rats to feed each cat each day. The rats in turn will be fed on the carcasses of the cats we skin. This will give each rat a quarter of a cat per day. You can see by this that the business is a clean operation . . . self-supporting, and really automatic throughout. The cats will eat the rats, and the rats will eat the cats, and we will get all the skins!!

Eventually, it is our hope to cross cats with snakes, because the resulting mutation would SKIN ITSELF twice a year. This would save the labor cost of skinning, as well as give us two skins for each "cat."

If the above program is not of interest to you, I would be one of the first to understand your hesitancy . . .

I don't know about you, but I have had opportunities for investments that have not been much better than this joke. But the sad thing is that when you compare the earthly investments we make of our time, talent, and wealth with the truly valuable eternal investments, most of our investments are but a joke.

In the parable of the unjust steward (Luke 16:1-3) Jesus teaches plainly that faithful stewardship requires that we be wise with a godly shrewdness. There are ways to invest that will bring lasting and valuable returns. We can invest in what Jesus will consider worthy of reward, the kingdom of heaven. Jesus said, "Again, the kingdom of heaven is like treasure hidden in a field, which a man found and hid, and for joy over it he goes and sells all that he has and buys that field. Again, the kingdom of heaven is like a merchant seeking beautiful pearls, who, when he had found one pearl of great price, went and sold all that he had and bought it" (Matthew 13:44-46).

How can we tell what is really important to Jesus? The Bible gives us "insider information" that prepares us for what is going to happen in the future by giving us the specifics of what will really count with God.

TEN PRINCIPLES OF WISE SPIRITUAL INVESTMENT

1. *Invest in the lives of those who minister the word.* In Galatians Paul emphasized the importance of supporting those in the ministry. Paul connected what a man sows in the form of giving and what he reaps in the sight of God—an apparent allusion to the judgment seat: "Let him who is taught the word share in all good things with him who teaches. Do not be deceived, God is not mocked; for whatever a man sows, that he will also reap" (Galatians 6:6-7).

2. *Minister to those in need.* Jesus made this basis for reward clear: "And whoever gives one of these little ones only a cup of cold water in the name of a disciple, assuredly, I say to you, he shall by no means lose his reward" (Matthew 10:42).

Those who minister to the needs of others will receive rewards. If as a disciple of Jesus, implying that it is in the name of Christ, you give a cup of cold water to someone who is thirsty, you can certainly count on a reward from Jesus. If you help to feed someone who is hungry or if you minister to someone who is hurting and needs to talk to a good listener, you will have reward. The Lord does not forget such things. "For God is not unjust to forget your work and labor of love which you have shown toward His name, in that you have ministered to the saints, and do minister" (Hebrews 6:10).

There are rewards for even very little things we do for others.

3. *Sacrifice to follow Christ.* In Matthew 19 Jesus is asked and responds to a question concerning sacrifices made for following Him:

Then Peter answered and said to Him, "See, we have left all and followed You. Therefore what shall we have?" So Jesus said to them, "Assuredly I say to you, that in the regeneration, when the

Son of Man sits on the throne of His glory, you who have followed Me will also sit on twelve thrones, judging the twelve tribes of Israel. And everyone who has left houses or brothers or sisters or father or mother or wife or children or lands, for My name's sake, shall receive a hundredfold, and inherit everlasting life." (Matthew 19:27-29)

When the disciples told Jesus that they had sacrificed everything to follow Him, He responded by saying that if they had sacrificed their relationship with their families, their parents, or their children—and did it for His sake—they would receive a reward for it one hundred times greater than what they had given up. Do not think that sacrifice for the sake of Christ will go unnoticed.

4. *Give without fanfare.* In the Sermon on the Mount Jesus gave clear instructions about the practice we should follow when we give. In those instructions is a truth about rewards: "Take heed that you do not do your charitable deeds before men, to be seen by them. Otherwise you have no reward from your Father in heaven. . . . When you do a charitable deed, do not let your left hand know what your right hand is doing, that your charitable deed may be in secret; and your Father who sees in secret will Himself reward you openly" (Matthew 6:1, 3-4).

Jesus promises treasure or reward in heaven for giving without fanfare. Be sure that your giving is done in such a way that you do not expect other people to honor you for your giving. If you try to get honor and respect for your giving, then the Lord says you have already received your reward here on earth.

5. *Accept abuse for the sake of Christ.* At the close of the Beatitudes Jesus said: "Blessed are you when they revile and persecute you, and say all kinds of evil against you falsely for My sake. Rejoice and be exceedingly glad, for great is your reward in heaven, for so they persecuted the prophets who were before you" (Matthew 5:11-12). Those who suffer abuse for their commitment to Jesus Christ will not be kept from reward.

6. *Pray in secret.* In the Sermon on the Mount Jesus spoke about the way we should pray: "And when you pray, you shall not be like the hypocrites. For they love to pray standing in the synagogues and on the corners of the streets, that they may be seen by men. Assuredly, I say to you, they have their reward. But you, when you pray, go into your room, and when you have shut your door, pray to your Father who is in the secret place; and your Father who sees in secret will reward you openly" (Matthew 6:5-6).

If we make our prayer life a personal thing between us and God that no one else in the world knows about, if we don't brag about it but see to it that it remains precious and special between us and God, He will reward us. The God who sees you in secret will reward you openly.

7. *Engage in spiritual activity without fanfare.* Jesus taught that spiritual or religious activity should be done without fanfare: "When you fast, do not be like the hypocrites, with a sad countenance. For they disfigure their faces that they may appear to men to be fasting. Assuredly, I say to you, they have their reward. But you, when you fast, anoint your head and wash your face, so that you do not appear to men to be fasting, but to your Father who is in the secret place; and your Father who sees in secret will reward you openly" (Matthew 6:16-18).

It is probable that we are expected to apply this exhortation to more than fasting—to any kind of spiritual exercise. Don't engage in any spiritual activity as a way of attempting to get attention from others.

On one occasion a number of years ago I got away for a week of study, prayer, and fasting. When I returned, I let other people know what a great time I had had. It is likely that by doing so I eliminated any kind of future reward for fasting at that time. True, I got a lot of studying done, but because I drew attention to my spiritual exercise, it probably was worthless in terms of spiritual rewards.

8. *Love your enemies by being willing to help them.* In Luke 6 Jesus spoke about the attitude we should have toward

our enemies: "But love your enemies, do good, and lend, hoping for nothing in return; and your reward will be great, and you will be sons of the Highest. For He is kind to the unthankful and evil" (v. 35).

Jesus' love ethic was practical. He taught that we should extend love even to our enemies. To underscore how strongly He felt about our doing that, He promised great reward.

9. *Give hearty service to the Lord and not just to please men.* Our service is to the Lord, not just to men: "And whatever you do, do it heartily, as to the Lord and not to men, knowing that from the Lord you will receive the reward of the inheritance; for you serve the Lord Christ" (Colossians 3:23-24).

The idea of rewards is linked not just to that which is "religious" but to all that we do in life. As we serve Christ on the job, we should do it with zest, desiring to do the best job we know how to do. Whatever we do—teaching, banking, counseling, mothering—we should work as unto the Lord. If you do your job, and do it well, committed always to a high level of work ethic because you love God and believe it is right for the Christian to do well, then the Lord promises that reward is a part of your inheritance in eternity.

10. *Entertain those who cannot repay you.* When you entertain others, it should be out of unselfish motives: "Then He also said to him who invited Him, When you give a dinner or a supper, do not ask your friends, your brothers, your relatives, nor your rich neighbors, lest they also invited you back, and you be repaid. But when you give a feast, invite the poor, the maimed, the lame, the blind. And you will be blessed, because they cannot repay you; for you shall be repaid at the resurrection of the just" (Luke 14:12-14).

Most of what we do for others is aimed at achieving some personal goal or desire. We give Christmas gifts to those we know will give back to us. We have people over for dinner, expecting to be invited back later. Jesus says the most valuable kind of giving and entertaining is that which helps those who cannot respond in kind to us.

BE A WISE INVESTOR

We spend too much of our time planning the purchase of houses, cars, and electronic gadgets and setting up investment portfolios. We would be wiser to focus our attention on investing in the lives of others and serving the Lord more effectively. Be a wise investor!

11

Negative Judgment at the *Bema*

Up to this point we have spoken primarily of positive rewards in the presence of Christ. However, we will not only be rewarded for the good in our lives at the *bema* but will have to face Jesus' response to the useless and sinful realities as well.

INDICATIONS OF NEGATIVE JUDGMENT AT THE *BEMA*

Those who address the issue of a negative aspect to the *bema* judgment usually fall into one of two camps. On the one hand are those who only suggest the possibility of a negative, judgmental aspect and soften the many references to Christ's future judgment of believers. On the other are those who overstate the negative aspects of the *bema* judgment. It is the goal of this examination of the major texts on the subject to add light and balance to the discussion.

Certainly, any honest student of the doctrine of the *bema* must recognize that there are passages that point to the presence of a negative aspect in the believer's judgment. One of the key passages on the *bema*, Romans 14, directly raises the issue: "But why do you judge your brother? Or why should you show contempt for your brother? For we shall all stand before the judgment seat of Christ. For it is written: 'As I live, says the Lord, every knee shall bow to Me, and every tongue shall confess to

God.' So then each of us shall give account of himself to God" (Romans 14:10-12). Paul clearly declares that every one of us will have to give account of his life to Christ. That certainly implies the possibility of negative things in our lives that we will need to explain to Christ.

Visualize yourself in the presence of Christ. He demands, "Do you acknowledge what you did on this occasion? Why did you do it? Did you not have enough information to understand that I explicitly said I did not want you to do that? Why was your personal comfort more important to you than serving Me? Why did you claim credit for what I did for and through you? Can you explain these filthy, self-centered thoughts?" The Scriptures are transparent. We will have to give account of our lives to Christ.

The other key *bema* passage is 2 Corinthians 5. In this passage Paul is even more direct: "For we must all appear before the judgment seat of Christ, that each one may receive the things done in the body, according to what he has done, whether *good or bad*" (2 Corinthians 5:10, italics added). Galatians 6:6-10 likewise speaks of reaping what we sow. That reaping may be not only in life but in eternity.

In 2 Timothy 1:16-18 Paul refers to special mercy from the Lord for the house of Onesiphorus in "that day" (in the context of referring to the day of Christ's coming and judgment of His own). If there were no possibility of negative judgment at the *bema,* why would mercy be needed beyond that which is the direct benefit of the cross through salvation? In Matthew 5:7, when Jesus promised that those who show mercy will receive mercy, He thereby implied that we will need mercy. That is in contrast to the warning that we will be judged with the same kind of judgment that we have measured out to others (Matthew 7:1-2).

The writer of the epistle to the Hebrews warns us of the danger of the willful sin of turning away from the Christ who sanctified us, leaving us vulnerable to God's fiery indignation (Hebrews 10:26-27).[1] Hebrews also declares that it is "a fearful thing to fall into the hands of the living God." Paul declares in

2 Corinthians 5:11 that he had a godly fear in the expectation of the coming *bema.*

In another general epistle, James warns teachers that they will receive the stricter judgment (James 4:1). Similarly, some expositors suggest that the book of Revelation teaches that a believer could be harmed, though not destroyed, by the second death (2:11).

From these references it seems to me that God wants us to realize there is a serious and fearful side to the *bema* judgment.

One additional passage bears mentioning. Colossians 3:24-25 appears to warn that the *bema* will include not only inheritance rewards but also judgment for wrong done in life. Paul says that not only will obedient slaves receive the reward of the inheritance but that "he who does wrong will be repaid for the wrong which he as done, and there is no partiality." The literal translation of this passage is "the one doing evil or unjustly will be recompensed for the evil or injustice he did." I personally doubt that this particular passage is relevant to the present discussion of negative judgment against believers at the *bema.* Instead, I believe that Paul is encouraging persecuted Christian slaves with the truth that any persecuting master will be judged by the Lord. The Lord, Paul says, is not impressed by the master's status as slave owner, for Christ has no partiality in his dealings with men.

Part of my reason for saying that Colossians 3:24-25 is not relevant to the *bema* judgment has to do with the context of the passage. In the context Christian slaves and masters are always referred to in the second person (you), whereas verse 25 is in the third person (he), thus implying that Paul is promising that Christ will not only reward slaves who are obedient to their evil masters but will make sure that what their evil masters do will follow them all the way to their judgment.

Other facts also leave the impression that Paul is referring to unbelieving masters: the phrase "without respect of persons" is used in the parallel passage in Ephesians 6 to refer to masters; the reference in the literal translation to "the one doing evil or unjustly'" seems more likely to refer to an unbeliever (Acts 24:1-5; 1 Corinthians 6:1, 9; 1 Peter 3:18; and 2 Peter 2:9);

and, finally, passages such as 2 Thessalonians 1:3-10 teach that the persecuting unbeliever will be condemned at Christ's coming, whereas the coming of Christ means glory to Christ in the believer. Thus it is unlikely that Paul has any negative judgment of the Christian in mind in Colossians 3:24-25.

Whether or not one interprets Colossians 3:25 to teach that we will be judged for the evil we have done, from the other passages mentioned above one truth is inescapable: when we stand before Christ at the *bema,* He will evaluate and respond to the bad in our lives as well as to the good.

RELATIONSHIP OF THE *BEMA* TO JUSTIFICATION

The New Testament is consistent in its teaching that we are justified, and thus forgiven of all sin when we trust Christ. Therefore, one may aptly inquire as to whether any sins will appear at the *bema,* since they have been removed from us as far as the east is from the west.

In the sense that our sins have been totally paid for by Christ relative to the demands of God's holy law, yes, they will never appear again on the divine court docket. As a result you can be assured that you will live forever; you will have a home with Christ forever; you will have access into the holy throne room of God. Ultimately, you will have every tear dried—every sadness wiped away, and you will share in the church's dominion over the entire creation forever. Nevertheless, though our actions that are legal transgressions may well be forgiven by the divine court, our Lord will still require a family reckoning.

NEGATIVE RECOMPENSE AT THE *BEMA*

Even though our sins will certainly be a part of the evaluation at the *bema,* the kind of response to our sins and other failures will be quite different from that which will be experienced by the unbeliever at the great white throne judgment. Hell, purgatory, or any other kind of punishment is not in view at the *bema.* Paul makes it clear that there is no condemnation to those who are in Christ Jesus (Romans 8:1). The New Testament also clarifies just what kind of negative results issue from Jesus' evaluation of our sin and failure at the *bema*. Specifically, there are two ways the Bible describes the negative recompense we might receive: loss of rewards (along with grief over loss) and shame.

LOSS AT THE *BEMA*

First Corinthians 3:15*a* describes the process of the *bema* judgment and warns: "If anyone's work is burned, he will suffer loss; but he himself will be saved." The *bema* judgment will certainly leave the foolish, earthly minded believer without the rewards announced to others. Those who failed to persevere in their faith in the promises of God will miss the experience of millennial rest (Hebrews 3; 4). Some who became stagnant in their walk with God will not be able to fully participate in the inheritance provided for them (Hebrews 6:12), and they will miss the special entrance into the kingdom provided for Christians who have developed godly character (2 Peter 1:5-11). Those who turned their backs on Christ, His people, and confidence in the promises of God will forfeit "*great* reward" (Hebrews 10:19-35, italics added). Some who started well in their Christian life but gave up when the going got tough will discover that they have lost the inheritance of their birthright blessings (Hebrews 12:1-17).

Others will discover that they have forfeited incorruptible crowns through their unwillingness to serve the Lord or because of some brief moments of selfish indulgence (1 Corinthians 9:26-27). Many will find that they really *could* have "taken it with them," if only they had invested in heavenly treasure (Matthew 6:19-20). Some who were given great talent, wealth, education, or opportunity but thoughtlessly and selfishly squandered those gifts from God will find much of their eternal honor and responsibility eliminated (Matthew 25:14-30). Those who selfishly caused division or any kind of hurt to the church will face God's indignation and lose much reward (1 Corinthians 3:16, 17).

Sadly, there will be those who will lose some of their reward because they foolishly followed a false teacher. A number of years ago I led a young Jewish man to Christ. Shortly after he was saved he was duped into joining a cult. For ten years he lived and worked for that group. Finally, when the Jim Jones massacre occurred, he was struck with the parallels between the cult he was in, the Children of God, and that of Jim Jones. It shook him to his senses, and he left the cult. As we talked together later, I was painfully aware that this young man had thrown away ten years of his life. The apostle John warned of such loss: "For many deceivers have gone out into the world who do not confess Jesus Christ as coming in the flesh. This is a deceiver and an antichrist. Look to yourselves, that we do not lose those things we worked for, but that we may receive a full reward" (2 John 7-8).

There is another major reason why many may possibly lose rewards even though they have consistently given to charity, prayed regularly, and carried out religious activities sacrificially. Jesus warns that such activities, when done for the purpose of gaining recognition before men, will bring no eternal recognition before God (Matthew 6:1-18).

On the other hand, the term translated "loss" in 1 Corinthians 3:15 is also used in Philippians 3, where Paul emphasizes his commitment to serve Christ in his personal race toward the goal of the *bema,* even if he suffers great loss in this life. In other words, often we must choose as to where we want the loss and where we want the gain—here and now or later in the messianic kingdom: "But what things were gain to me, these I have counted loss for Christ. But indeed I also count all things loss for the excellence of the knowledge of Christ Jesus my Lord, for whom I have suffered the loss of all things, and count them as rubbish, that I may gain Christ" (Philippians 3:7-8).

GRIEF OVER LOSS

With all that is said in terms of warnings about loss of rewards in the Scriptures, it is obvious that the empty-handed believer at the *bema* will experience a deep sense of loss—even grief—over what he has lost, and grief over the sobering realization that he cannot now repent. The writer of the epistle to the Hebrews alludes to this in his reference to Esau, the fraternal twin brother of Jacob. Because Esau was a "profane" man who lived only for the present and for earthly comforts, he sold his birthright to Jacob for one meal. He viewed the promises of God to his father, Isaac, and his grandfather, Abraham, as worthless. "Afterward, when he wanted to inherit the blessing, he was rejected, for he found no place for repentance, though he sought it diligently with tears" (Hebrews 12:17).

Perhaps some of the parables of our Lord refer to this grief also. On five different occasions Jesus described people in His parables as being so grieved by their exclusion from the blessings of the kingdom that they wept and gnashed their teeth (Matthew 8:5-14; 22:11-15; 24:45-51; 25:14-31; and Luke 13:22-31). Although most of those passages are directed to the people of Israel and do not directly describe the event of the *bema* of the church, they do seem to indicate that a servant of Christ can suffer such great loss at our Lord's coming again as to bring about weeping and gnashing of teeth.

SHAME

In his first letter the apostle John warned believers concerning the possibility of being ashamed at the coming of Christ: "And now, little children, abide in Him, that when He appears, we may have confidence and not be ashamed before Him at His coming" (1 John 2:28). Assuming that John had in mind the great event of the *bema* that immediately follows the coming of Christ for His church at the rapture, John was admonishing us to live in such a way that what we are doing will not be a great embarrassment when Jesus lays our lives bare for evaluation.

There are two ways that we can appear before Jesus when he comes. We can come into His presence with confidence. The book of Hebrews talks of a bold confidence to enter the presence of God. Or we can shrink in shame from the presence of our Lord. In 1 John, the apostle John exhorted his readers: "Beloved, now we are children of God; and it has not yet been revealed what we shall be, but we know that when He is revealed, we shall be like Him, for we shall see Him as He is. And everyone who has this hope in Him purifies himself, just as He is pure" (1 John 3:2-3). John appears to be telling us that there is the possibility of a person's being impure, of being involved in that which is a disgrace for a child of God. He will experience great shame in the presence of Christ.

The negative part of the *bema* judgment may be similar to the time when Peter stood near Christ during His trial. Jesus looked over at the man who had denied Him three times and He convicted him with the eyes of betrayed love—not with vindictive words, but with the gentle reproach of someone who truly understood Peter's human fears. His will not be an antagonistic legal judgment by someone who desires to punish us. It will be the loving judgment of the One who died for us.

PREPARATION FOR THE *BEMA* JUDGMENT

In view of the possibility of a negative experience at the coming of Christ and our appearance in His presence for evaluation, how might we prepare for that great day so that it is a time of rejoicing and celebration and not a time of grief over loss and shame? I would like to suggest two major preparations: establishing godly plans and priorities and maintaining purity and holiness.

PLANNING AND PRIORITIES

In Matthew 25 Jesus taught of the importance of wise investment. We may infer from that emphasis that the faithful and wise steward plans well and sets his priorities wisely. Make sure that your life really counts—counts for eternity—so that at the *bema* you will not suffer loss. Invest in the lives of others and use your gifts to the glory of God.

PURITY AND HOLINESS

In 1 John 3:3 the apostle John exhorted those who had their hope fixed on the coming of Jesus to purify themselves, even as Jesus is pure. How is that possible? Not only do we have current sins to deal with, we have garbage in the past to clear away. None of us is sinless, as John makes clear: "If we say that we have no sin, we deceive ourselves, and the truth is not in us. . . . If we say that we have not sinned, we make Him a liar, and His word is not in us" (1 John 1:8-10).

But I have good news. It is possible for us to have God's record of our sins cleansed in advance of the *bema*.

Our situation is something like that of a defendant in a trial who goes free because taped evidence scheduled to be used against him has been erased. God personally "erases" the "tapes" of our sins when we present them to Him through confession. Thus we can have our lives totally purified. John described this wonderful promise by saying, "If we walk in the light, as He is in the light, we have fellowship with one another, and the blood of Jesus Christ His Son cleanses us from all sin" (1 John 1:7). Then in a more specific way he restates the promise: "If we confess our sins, He is faithful and just to forgive us our sins, and to cleanse us from all unrighteousness" (v. 9).

That is wonderful! Not only can we be assured of forgiveness for the sins of which God is currently convicting us, but we can know also that He cleanses us from *all* unrighteousness. John was saying, "Step into the light. Let the Lord shine on you with the light of His Word. Then be responsive when the Word tells you that you have committed wrong. Acknowledge it—and move on."

We prepare to meet Jesus as holy vessels by keeping short accounts with God. If we judge our own sin and acknowledge it to God, He doesn't have to judge it later. The same principle is found in 1 Corinthians 11 in the context of self-examination at the communion table: "For if we would judge ourselves, we would not be judged" (1 Corinthians 11:31).

A number of years ago I came to know an elderly, retired Baptist preacher by the name of P. C. James. His two daughters were members of our church, but at that time he was the hospital visitor for another church. Occasionally I would offer to be his driver so that I could get to know him better. What a blessing for a young pastor!

One day I received word that Dr. James, then in his eighties, was in the hospital facing surgery and might not recover. Immediately I hastened to see him. When I walked into the hospital room I noticed that he was quite agitated, so I began to try to encourage him in the face of death.

He stopped me abruptly, "Joe, you don't know what you're talking about. I'm not afraid to die. In fact I've been looking forward to it. My problem is that I just bawled out my nurse, and I don't want to appear in the presence of Jesus with that on my conscience. Would you pray with me that I would have the opportunity not only to confess my anger to the Lord but also to see the nurse in the morning before I go into surgery, so that I can ask her forgiveness?"

Dr. James believed in keeping short accounts with God. That is the way to keep ourselves pure in preparation to meet Jesus.

Note

1. I recognize that some would interpret this warning in Hebrews as directed to those in the Hebrew congregation who professed to be believers but were in fact yet unsaved. That interpretation seems to me to contradict the argument of the book as a whole, namely, that the author is challenging the Hebrew Christians to persevere in order to receive eternal rewards, described as inheritance and rest.

Part 3

THE LIFE THAT WINS

12

The Wreath-Crowns

If we are really serious about preparing to meet Jesus at the *bema,* we should "go for the gold." The top awards in the modern Olympic games are the gold medals. The parallel in New Testament times were the wreath-crowns. The Bible gives us much instruction on how to "go" for those crowns. In this and the next four chapters we will summarize the biblical doctrine of the wreath-crowns and attempt to provide additional teachings that can help the believer strive for the best.

THE *STEPHANOS* AND THE *DIADEM*

In the New Testament there are two words for "crown": *stephanos* and *diadem.* The *stephanos* was a wreath-crown, and the *diadem* was the royal crown.

In the ancient Middle East, the turban worn by Persian monarchs was called a *diadem.* It was quite different from the diadem we normally think of when we speak of the regalia worn by a European king. In its basic meaning the word *diadem* refers to something that is "wrapped around." In the Middle East, the diadem could be the royal turban itself, which was made by wrapping a long cloth about the head to form a head-dress, or it could refer to a colored ribbon, usually blue and white, tied around the turban to indicate royalty. When a king conquered a kingdom, he the might require the vanquished king to bow before him as he placed his foot on his neck as a symbol of victory. The victorious king might also take the ribbon from the conquered king's turban and add it to his own.

If a man ruled over many kingdoms, he could be crowned with "many crowns," or diadems. We sing the hymn "Crown Him with Many Crowns." This hymn probably should not be thought of as a picture of placing a number of golden crowns on Jesus' head but rather as a picture of crowning an oriental monarch with a turban on which had been wrapped ribbons representing every nation of the earth, thus acknowledging Jesus as King of kings and Lord or lords.

In the New Testament, *diadem* is used to refer to the kind of crown only Jesus gets. Believers do not get diadems.

The *stephanos,* or wreath-crown, was quite a different kind of crown. It was a collection of branches woven together and placed on the head of a person who had won a victory. It was the victor's crown. After a battle a general might receive a *stephanos* as a symbol that he had won a battle. Such a practice has its parallels even in more modern times. For example, one entire wall in the Arc de Triomphe in Paris is covered with bronze wreath-crowns in honor of officers in Napoleon's army.

In ancient times a leader might take a wreath-crown and put it on his head prior to battle to indicate to his troops that he planned to win. Thus Jesus wears the *stephanos* as He prepares for Armageddon and His final, triumphant second advent.

The *stephanos* was awarded at the Panhellenic games, such as the Olympics. When a person won his race, he received the winner's reward—a garland of wild olive leaves, pine needles, laurel, or parsley. Such a crown carried a great deal of significance for the winner. It was the medal of honor, the gold medal, the blue ribbon, the first place trophy. It was the very best award you could win. It not only meant that you had won, but that you also had many special benefits coming to you when you returned home. (See further explanation of these benefits in chapter 3.)

So the New Testament *stephanos* was a high, exalted emblem of victory. The New Testament believer receives other rewards, but the *stephanos* is reserved for being a winner. It is the most important reward reserved in heaven for the Christian.

Though some suggest that there are five wreath-crowns referred to in the New Testament, I believe that there are four. They are the crown of righteousness, the crown of life, the crown of joy, and the crown of glory. First Corinthians 9:25, which refers to an imperishable crown, should be taken as a summary statement concerning all of the crowns: "And everyone who competes for the prize is temperate in all things. Now they do it to obtain a perishable crown, but we for an imperishable crown."

The crowns we receive when we appear before Jesus will not fall apart. They will last for eternity. Perhaps they will be hung in a special hall in heaven like those of Napoleon's generals in the Arc de Triomphe. Or perhaps they will be a part of our personal homes, magnifying the glory that is to be revealed. Then again we may be able to wear the crowns as continual expressions of praise to Jesus.

One crown will be given for people we win to Christ, and in fact the people that are won to Christ are themselves called crowns. Perhaps we will both wear crowns and have people present throughout eternity who serve as continual reminders of the work of grace in which God gave us a part to play. In any case, Paul is clear: the crown rewards are not perishable—they will last forever.

THE CROWN OF RIGHTEOUSNESS

The first crown is the *wreath-crown of righteousness.* This crown is mentioned in 2 Timothy 4 and refers to the crown awarded for finishing the race of life righteously, with our eyes on Jesus, excitedly anticipating His return. "I have fought the good fight, I have finished the race, I have kept the faith. Finally, there is laid up for me the *crown of righteousness,* which the Lord, the righteous Judge, will give to me on that Day, and not to me only but also to all who have loved His appearing" (2 Timothy 4:7-8, italics added).

Paul here gives three related traits of people who are excited about seeing Jesus at the rapture and the *bema,* those who "love his appearing." First, though they may fail, they continue to struggle to compete ("fight the good fight"). Second, they continue to follow Jesus and carry out the ministry course designed for them ("finish the race"). Third, they live lives that are not "disqualified" (1 Corinthians (9:26-27) by moral compromise but are characterized by "keeping the faith" (to "keep the faith" may refer to an Olympic athlete's commitment to follow the rules). All such people are promised the crown of righteousness. Jesus seems to be teaching a similar thought in Luke 12:35-40.[1]

THE CROWN OF LIFE

The second crown, the *wreath-crown of life,* is referred to in two different places. That fact indicates that the mention of the crown of life in the New Testament was not an isolated figure of speech used by only one apostle but was a technical reward term. Both James and John used the term (James 1:12; Revelation 2:20), and they used it in the same way:

> Blessed is the man who endures temptation; for when he has been proved, he will receive the *crown of life* which the Lord has promised to those who love Him. (James 1:12, italics added)

> Do not fear any of those things which you are about to suffer. Indeed, the devil is about to throw some of you into prison, that you may be tested, and you will have tribulation ten days. Be faithful until death, and I will give you the *crown of life.* (Revelation 2:10, italics added)

The crown of life is the crown given to those who persevere under trial, the ones who "hang in there" all the way to the end, even in times of suffering. This crown is especially relevant to those who suffer persecution and martyrdom for the sake of Christ: "Blessed are you when they revile and persecute you, and say all kinds of evil against you falsely for My sake. Rejoice and be exceedingly glad, for great is your reward in heaven, for so they persecuted the prophets who were before you" (Matthew 5:11-12).

THE CROWN OF JOY

The third crown is the *wreath-crown of joy.* The crown of joy is referred to in 1 Thessalonians and also in Philippians, where Paul describes the crown of joy in terms of those people he has led to Christ:

> For what is our hope, or joy, or *crown of rejoicing?* Is it not even you in the presence of our Lord Jesus Christ at His coming? For you are our glory and joy. (1 Thessalonians 2:19-20, italics added)

> Therefore, my beloved and longed-for brethren, my *joy and crown,* so stand fast in the Lord, beloved. (Philippians 4:1, italics added)

Apparently this crown is made of the people to whom we have ministered, especially in the area of evangelism. Perhaps we will have both a symbol (a crown) on the heads of our glorified bodies as well as the enjoyment of having with us in heaven forever the people to whom we have ministered.

THE CROWN OF GLORY

The fourth crown is the one found in 1 Peter 5, the *wreath-crown of glory.* Speaking to the elders of the church, Peter exhorts them: "Shepherd the flock of God which is among you, serving as overseers, not by constraint but willingly, not for dishonest gain but eagerly; nor as being lords over those entrusted to you, but being examples to the flock; and when the Chief Shepherd appears you will receive the *crown of glory* that does not fade away" (1 Peter 5:2-4, italics added).

Having served over twenty-five years with many different elders in a variety of difficult situations, I can understand why the Lord would make a special award for church leaders. Often hard decisions have to be made in confidence for the good of the flock, and often criticism follows. Hours of time and energy are poured into planning, budgeting, personnel problems, church discipline issues, and personal ministry to individuals in the congregation—often with little or no appreciation from others.

I have seen good elders and poor elders. Some elders continually pushed the doctrine of elder-rule on the congregation, lording it over the flock, whereas others demonstrated loving patience and concern. Some elders who served as staff pastors were more concerned about their careers and making money than about the needs of God's people, whereas others demanded nothing and accepted little for their labor because of their love for the Lord and their flock. Many elders will receive this crown, but some will not.

CONCLUSION

Wreath-crowns are the most important rewards on which our Lord wanted us to focus. We do not know for certain if there are crowns other than the four mentioned in Scripture. But we do know that those four are the ones the Lord wanted us to know about in order to understand what in our lives is really important to God. The *crown of righteousness* focuses our attention on the importance of carrying out the ministry God has designed for us, persevering righteously to the end of our course. The *crown of life* reminds us of the importance of always entrusting ourselves to the arms of our beloved Lord as we endure suffering. The *crown of joy* emphasizes the great need to minister the gospel to others. And the the *crown of glory* is an encouragement to accept and carry out the leadership responsibilities we have been given in the life of the church.

In the next four chapters we will consider specific biblical teaching that can enhance our capability of attaining the four wreath-crowns.

Note

1. Jesus seems to be teaching a similar thought in Luke 12:35-40.

13

The Crown of Righteousness and Divine Guidance

Finishing the course God has designed for each of us carries with it the hope of great reward—*the wreath-crown of righteousness.* It is important, therefore, to be aware of God's leading in our lives. This chapter focuses on the doctrine of divine guidance.

Some suggest today that God does not have a specific plan for the individual's life. They teach that the only level at which the believer is to consider understanding the will of God for his life concerns the moral will of God as revealed objectively in Scripture. But in 2 Timothy 4:6-8 Paul described his life as a race and spoke of having had a particular course to fulfill. Furthermore, in verse 5 he reminded Timothy that he too had a specific ministry to carry out: "But you be watchful in all things, endure afflictions, do the work of an evangelist, fulfill your ministry" (2 Timothy 4:5).

When Jesus completed the ministry that provided salvation through His suffering and death, He cried out, "It is finished." He had completed the earthly course set out for the Messiah. Likewise, John the Baptist had a course he finished in preparation for the coming of the Messiah (Acts 13:25).

It is striking that some time before he wrote 2 Timothy Paul spoke of planning to continue traveling to Jerusalem even though he knew that danger awaited him there, because he wanted to complete the life-plan God had for him. In his stirring message to the Ephesian elders just before his departure for Jerusalem he said: "But none of these things move me; nor do I count my life dear to myself, so that I may finish my race with joy, and the ministry which I received from the Lord Jesus, to testify to the gospel of the grace of God" (Acts 20:24).

At the conclusion of his life, Paul wrote that the crown of righteousness awaited him because he had finished the course (race) that God had planned for him: "For I am already being poured out as a drink offering, and the time of my departure is at hand. I have fought the good fight, I have finished the race, I have kept the faith. Finally, there is laid up for me the crown of righteousness, which the Lord, the righteous Judge, will give to me on that Day, and not to be only but also to all who have loved His appearing" (2 Timothy 4:6-9).

Certainly God has given each of us gifts enabling us to carry out meaningful service in the world and for the church, and He has in mind the best path for us to follow to most significantly serve Him.

How to Stay on Course

If each one of us has a course for his life and the crown of righteousness is reserved for finishing that course still eagerly awaiting the return of Jesus, then knowing how to stay on course is important.

FOLLOW THE SHEPHERD

There are different approaches to the subject of divine guidance. Some suggest that God has a road map He hides from us until we push the right spiritual button, at which time He reveals a little bit more of the plan He has for our lives. Others teach that God's only plan for us is that we live moral lives within His revealed moral will; thus decisions about our mates, our vocations, our schooling, our ministries, and our day-to-day activities are to be made freely without regard to finding God's will in these matters. Such decisions then become ones of wisdom only.

It seems to me that the truth lies halfway between those two positions. Divine guidance should be viewed as the leadership of a shepherd who leads daily, moment-by-moment. In John 10 Jesus specifically describes Himself as the "good shepherd," and the book of Hebrews uses the term *author* to describe His relationship to us. The word *author* is a translation of a Greek word meaning "leader of a file." Thus Jesus is the one who has gone before us and waits for us to follow. Such a view of our Lord's leadership is a comfort because it both assures us that He is leading and at the same time reminds us that we are sinful, unwise sheep continually in need of forgiveness, restoration, and leadership. No one but Jesus lived a life perfectly in the will of God, so that even if we could find the perfect plan for our lives (a road map) we could not follow it perfectly. The good news is that Jesus is leading us in spite of our failures.

How does He lead? He leads in three different ways. First, He leads through His revealed Word, the Bible. Second, He leads sovereignly—through providential circumstances—in spite of how much we understand about His life-plan for us. Third, He leads us by providing us directly with the direction He wants us to perceive and follow. This last form of leading is illustrated particularly in an incident that occurred in the life of Paul on his second missionary journey through Asia Minor. At a particular point in his travels the Holy Spirit gave him personal direction: "Now when they had gone through Phrygia and the region of Galatia, they were forbidden by the Holy Spirit to preach the word in Asia. After they had come to Mysia, they tried to go into Bithynia, but the Spirit did not permit them" (Acts 16:6-7).

HOW TO FOLLOW THE SHEPHERD

Five principles of divine guidance are especially helpful to keep in mind in learning how to follow the Shepherd.

Principle #1. Yield your life to the lordship of Christ

Paul teaches that the Christian who has experienced the mercy of God in salvation ought to yield to Christ as absolute Lord. In so doing he is able to live out a life that proves that God's will is good and acceptable and perfect: "I beseech you therefore, brethren, by the mercies of God, that you present your bodies a living sacrifice, holy, acceptable to God, which is your reasonable service. And do not be conformed to this world, but be transformed by the renewing of your mind, that you may prove what is that good and acceptable and perfect will of God" (Romans 12:1-2).

In a similar vein Jesus taught that one can be given understanding of the truthfulness of a particular teaching if he is willing to obey the truth when he hears it: "If anyone wants to do His will, he shall know concerning the doctrine, whether it is from God or whether I speak on My own authority" (John 7:17).

So our commitment to obey Jesus as Lord is the foundational issue that needs to be settled before we can hope to understand His leading in our lives.

Principle #2. Walk in wisdom

Once we have submitted our will to Christ's will, then the primary way that He leads us is through wisdom. An examination of the leadership of God in the early church reveals that the church usually made decisions based on wisdom. Paul specifically exhorts us to walk in wisdom: "See then that you walk circumspectly, not as fools but as wise, redeeming the time, because the days are evil. Therefore do not be unwise, but understand what the will of the Lord is" (Ephesians 5:15-17). This approach seems also to be taught in passages such as Romans 12:2 and Psalm 1.

The Bible is the primary source of wisdom. It is here that we learn many specific guidelines for making wise decisions. Here are a few of them:

1. *The Scriptural Principle: Do not do anything that directly contradicts scriptural principles.* A young Christian lady is

in love with a nonbelieving man and wants to marry him. She also wants to know the Lord's direction in the matter. In this case there is clear scriptural teaching. In 2 Corinthians 6:14 Scripture explicitly warns against being "unequally yoked" with unbelievers. Although the immediate context of the passage focuses on the linking of Christian ministry with unbelieving religious activities, the principle certainly could apply to any close association between believers and unbelievers, such as a marriage or business partnership that forces the believer to go in the wrong direction or at least limit his ability to fully serve Christ.

2. *The Ethical Principle: Do not do anything that is unethical.* Paul was quick to emphasize that his ministry was always carried out in an ethical manner: "You are witnesses, and God also, how devoutly and justly and blamelessly we behaved ourselves among you who believe " (1 Thessalonians 2:10).

A number of years ago I encountered a group called the Children of God, who claimed to be able to tell young men and women what God's will was—namely, to join their movement. I was able to steer one young man away from the group by noting that the group rationalized away their unethical activities by pointing to the greater goals of their ministry. Any activity that is unethical is not in the will of God.

3. *The Spiritual Desire Principle: God often leads us through the desires of our hearts when we are delighting in our relationship with Him.* The psalmist wrote, "Delight yourself also in the Lord, and He shall give you the desires of your heart" (Psalm 37:4). The implication of this verse of promise is that when we are delighting in Him the Lord will provide the kind of desires in our hearts that He is willing to provide to us. Thus indirectly this passage gives us an additional principle for divine guidance.

A number of years ago I counseled a young man who loved to compose music for the Lord but didn't think the Lord was leading him in it because he liked it too much. To the contrary, I would think that such a desire could well be the way the Lord was leading him.

4. *The Open Door Principle: When you are trying to see the Good Shepherd's leadership more clearly, attempt to go in a different direction and see if He opens the door of opportunity for you.* Often the Scriptures refer to this principle:

> For a great and effective door has opened to me, and there are many adversaries. (1 Corinthians 16:9)

> Furthermore, when I came to Troas to preach Christ's gospel, and a door was opened to me by the Lord, I had no rest in my spirit. (2 Corinthians 2:12-13)

> I know your works. See, I have set before you an open door, and no one can shut it. (Revelation 3:8)

God often opens opportunities before us and we need to be sensitive to His provision.

5. *The Authority Principle: As long as the direction is not directly contrary to Scripture, we are to obey the authority over us.* Paul tells us that in so doing we are doing the will of God: "Servants be obedient to those who are your masters according to the flesh, with fear and trembling, in sincerity of heart, as to Christ; not with eyeservice, as men-pleasers, but as servants of Christ, doing the will of God from the heart, with good will doing service, as to the Lord, and not to men" (Ephesians 6:5-7).

Many times we are faced with difficult decisions that can easily be determined by responding positively to those in authority over us. This principle has application to any authority structure: child to parent, citizen to government, employee to supervisor, student to teacher, wife to husband, or any other established relationship.

6. *The Mature Advice Principle: Often God speaks to us through the counsel of mature friends and family members.*

The book of Proverbs speaks of the value of such wisdom: "Where there is no counsel, the people fall; But in the multitude of counselors there is safety" (Proverbs 11:14).

As a young pastor, when I faced hard decisions I would find myself kneeling in prayer with the Hartfields. Elmer and Maurine Hartfield were older Christians in our church who had walked with our Lord for many years, and I was never disappointed at their warm and insightful counsel. When making major decisions, the Christian who desires to hear a word from God would do well to seek the counsel of others, especially that of mature Christians.

7. *The Meaningful Circumstance Principle: God sometimes supplements our prayer life and the other means of guidance through meaningful circumstances.* In Acts 10 and 11 Luke describes the way God led Peter to take the gospel to the gentiles at Caesarea. Peter had gone up to the roof of the house of Simon the tanner at Joppa, a few miles down the coast of the Mediterranean Sea from Caesarea. While in prayer Peter received a vision that taught him that God can make anything or anyone clean that He wants to. Right after the vision a meaningful circumstance occurred: two messengers sent from Cornelius, a Roman centurion of Caesarea, came to Simon's door asking for Peter to come to Caesarea to speak to his household. The circumstance of the presence of the messengers from an unclean gentile was meaningful to Peter in light of the vision that he had just seen.

This form of guidance should not be confused with the practice of praying for signs and omens, a practice that often borders on superstition and magic, rather than divine guidance.

The closest thing to praying for signs in Scripture is Gideon's prayer in Judges 6:36-40. After God had already given direction to him, Gideon still wanted some reassurance of God's presence with him. He placed a fleece of wool on the ground and left it overnight, asking the Lord to cover it with dew while leaving the ground dry. Then on a subsequent night Gideon asked the Lord to reverse the process and leave the fleece dry and the ground wet. In both cases God obliged, and Gideon went forth to fight a massive army of 135,000 men with a small band of 300 men. With a clear assurance from God, Gideon won a great victory.

I would conclude from Gideon's experience that at times when the Lord is leading us to do something that requires great faith He is willing to give us a special sign for reassurance, to confirm earlier communication of His direction to us. However, that is quite different from trying to manipulate God to give us circumstantial signs regularly so that we can avoid the hard work of applying the other principles of divine guidance.

8. *The "Course of Life" Principle: Understanding the Lord's leading in our lives for the future is often made clearer when we see the future in relationship to God's leading in the past.* Paul seems to have had this principle in mind when he made the difficult decision to go to Jerusalem at the end of his third missionary journey. "But none of these things moved me; nor do I count my life dear to myself, so that I may finish my race [course] with joy, and the ministry which I received from the Lord Jesus, to testify to the gospel of the grace of God" (Acts 20:24). Paul was directed by his understanding of his calling to a particular ministry and to a particular course of life. It is helpful in making hard decisions about the future to evaluate the spiritual gifts the Lord has given us and the way he has led us thus far in the course of each of our lives.

Principle #3. Respond to the conviction of the Holy Spirit

Too often we Christians are prone to ignore the subjective element in the life of the Christian. Perhaps we have been turned off by those who frequently claim that "God told them" to do certain things just because they happened to have a particular feeling about it. Nonetheless, there is certainly biblical precedent for the inner conviction and urging of the Holy Spirit.

Jesus taught that the Holy Spirit would have a ministry of conviction of sin, righteousness, and judgment (John 16:8), and that He would guide us into all truth (John 16:13). So it is not surprising to find Paul changing the whole course of his ministry based on the inner leadership of the Holy Spirit (Acts 16:6-8).

When the Holy Spirit thus directs us, it must be something deeper than just surface emotions. I would suggest that His leading usually takes the form of either pain in our consciences or the deep stirring of a burden in our souls.

Principle #4. Be open to the Lord's intrusion into your life

Both Peter and Paul were visited with dreams and visions. Peter began his ministry to the Gentiles because of a vision at Joppa. Paul passed by the province of Asia and its capital, Ephesus, and went on to Philippi where a beating and jail awaited him because he had seen a vision in Troas of a man from Macedonia pleading for him to come and help them. On the surface Paul made a bad choice, but it was in fact a part of the divine strategy: the first major move of the gospel to Europe.

Leading through visions has its dangers, though. Many false cults have been started by people who have claimed to have had visions from God. The wise approach, it seems to me, would be to view the visions or dreams of others with extreme caution, allowing time to verify the vision with Scripture and events.

Principle #5. Trust in the sovereignty of God

Once we have done the best we can to discern the Shepherd's leading through the other principles, we need to rest in His sovereign direction of our lives and the entire progress of history toward His planned goals. The book of Proverbs says it clearly and directly: "Trust in the Lord with all your heart, And lean not on your own understanding; in all your ways acknowledge Him, and He shall direct your paths" (Proverbs 3:5-6).

So, then, follow your Shepherd, the Lord Jesus Christ, and finish the course He has for you, looking expectantly and lovingly for the time when you will appear in His glorious presence.

14

The Crown of Life and Persevering under Trial

Going for the gold (the wreath-crown) not only involves finishing the ministry-course God has designed for us but also involves persevering under trial. The *crown of life* awaits the one who endures faithfully when he goes through suffering. "Blessed is the man who endures temptation; for when he has been proved, he will receive the crown of life which the Lord has promised to those who love Him" (James 1:12). The book of Revelation also reminds us of the importance of this reward: "Do not fear any of those things which you are about to suffer. Indeed, the devil is about to throw some of you into prison, that you may be tested, and you will have tribulation ten days. Be faithful until death, and I will give you the crown of life" (Revelation 2:10).

A Crown Accessible to All Christians

When Christians gather to pray for one another, and when they are truly honest with one another, they discover that all of them have problems and pain. Some trials have their roots in their relationships with their children or with their parents. Some Christians struggle with the result of childhood abuse.

Others have major problems in their marriages or in their businesses. Still others undergo persecution at work or at school because of their faith. Many Christians in this country have gone to jail for their stand on moral issues, and in many nations of the world large numbers of believers have faced and do face prison and death for their faith.

The book of Job puts it this way: "Man is born to trouble as the sparks fly upward" (5:7). Paul tells us that "all who live godly in Christ Jesus will suffer persecution" (2 Timothy 3:12). Opportunity to go for the crown of life is not hard to find.

THE PERSEVERING CHRISTIAN

The Greek word translated "perseverance" in the passage from James quoted above is *hupomeno. Meno* means "remain," and *hupo* means "under." The Greek term therefore carries the meaning "to remain bravely, constantly, under whatever the pressure is that has come into our lives."

In his *Institutes,* Calvin says, "Better to live in the way, than to run with swiftness out of it." It may not be easy, and it may not look like the persevering Christian is always a "victorious Christian." He may weep; he may be depressed; he may wrestle with his trust in God and his understanding of what it means to trust God, but he nevertheless *remains.*

I have a pastor friend whose wife was extremely ill and partially paralyzed for many years until she died. He, his sister-in-law, his three children, and many in his church took care of her at home, bearing a heavy burden from crisis to crisis for almost ten years. There were many times my friend felt depressed, hopeless, trapped, and angry with God. But through it all he continually returned to his Lord, trusting in His all-wise sovereignty. Recently as we visited together in the hospital, he shared one of his deepest desires. He said he wants to be so responsive to his Lord's leadership that he would be like a loving servant at his master's feet, ready and sensitive to obey even the slightest movement of his Lord's smallest finger.

A person who perseveres may stumble, he may hurt deeply, and he may cry out to God as King David did repeatedly in the Psalms, but ultimately he remains true to his Lord, returning to Him for comfort and hope.

HOW TO PERSEVERE UNDER TRIAL

In the first chapter of his epistle, James provides significant insight into the way a Christian can deal positively with suffering. There are three major ways the believer can be strengthened in the midst of suffering.

BY MAINTAINING AN ETERNAL PERSPECTIVE

One of the main ways the Bible provides strength in the midst of suffering is through the revelation of enough truth about the future to give us an eternal perspective. In the passages concerning the crown of life we are immediately forced to think about the future glorious day when pain and suffering will cease and when we will be commended and rewarded by our Lord. Paul also provides us with a striking contrast between our suffering and the future glory of our heavenly home:

> Therefore we do not lose heart. Even though our outward man is perishing, yet the inward man is being renewed day by day. For our light affliction, which is but a moment, is working for us a far more exceeding and eternal weight of glory, while we do not look at the things which are seen, but at the things which are not seen. For the things which are seen are temporary, but the things which are not seen are eternal. (2 Corinthians 4:16-18)

That must have been the attitude of the apostles after they had been beaten by the Sanhedrin for preaching Christ. "So they departed from the presence of the council, rejoicing that they were counted worthy to suffer shame for His name" (Acts 5:41). Paul also expressed an eternal perspective in his epistle to the Romans: "For I consider that the sufferings of this present time are not worthy to be compared with the glory which shall be revealed in us" (Romans 8:18).

Although suffering is hard, the Christian has the hope that it is only for the present—our brief sojourn on this planet. And the future beyond this life is filled not only with wonderful blessings but an enriched inheritance for those who suffer and remain steadfast in their commitment to Christ and love relationship with Him through the suffering.

BY RELYING ON GOD'S WISDOM IN THE FACE OF SUFFERING

The second way James tells us that the suffering Christian can be strengthened is through divinely provided wisdom. In the first chapter of James in the midst of a discussion of trials, James interjects a wonderful promise: "If any of you lacks wisdom, let him ask of God, who gives to all liberally and without reproach, and it will be given him" (James 1:5).

Why the sudden mention of wisdom? James understood that one of the greatest helps in facing a trial is having a better understanding of the bigger picture—of having God's point of view of events, of seeing His reasons for the suffering.

In one sense it is wrong to cry out to God, "Why?"—especially if we cry out in a defiant and challenging way. But it is right to ask God "Why?" in the sense of wanting to have a better understanding of what God is doing in our lives. The first cry *challenges* God's wisdom; the second cry *taps* His wisdom. James assures us that, if we ask God for wisdom, He will not respond with disdain or reproach, but will freely give it to us.

The promise given in James is similar to the promise given to the prophet Jeremiah when he had been arrested for preaching the truth: "Moreover the word of the Lord came to Jeremiah a second time, while he was still shut up in the court of the prison, saying, 'Thus says the Lord who made it, the Lord who formed it to establish it (the Lord is His name): "Call to Me, and I will answer you, and show you great and mighty things, which you do not know"'" (Jeremiah 33:1-3).

God promised Jeremiah that He would let him see things he had never known before. God was saying, "When you are in the pit, when things are not going your way, I will tell you enough so that you are able to handle the pain." Certainly this promise to Jeremiah has application to us as well, we who have the clear promise of the provision of divine wisdom in the midst of trials in the New Testament.

I do not believe that God normally gives us total understanding of why we suffer. We may never know fully why we have to experience suffering, never truly understand how good can come from our being hurt in some way. But I do believe that God does promise to give us part of the picture—enough to sustain us.

BY DISTINGUISHING BETWEEN CAUSES OF
AND DIVINE PURPOSES IN SUFFERING

It has strengthened me to know that the Bible teaches that God is not the cause of suffering for the believer though He is working out wonderful purposes through my suffering.

A number of years ago I received a telephone call from a couple who had come to know Christ in a church I had formerly pastored. Their thirteen-year-old son had been diagnosed with terminal cancer. I hurried to the hospital to be with them. As we talked in the hospital snack room, the mother leaned across the table and said to me, "I need to ask you a question that is really bothering me. Why? Why our child? He's a Christian. Both of us are Christians. His sister is a Christian. He has given his life to serve the Lord. Why?"

"There are no simple answers," I responded, "but I have been helped by a book by James Martin, *Suffering Man, Loving God.*" Some time later they told me that Martin's words had especially ministered to them. Here is a small segment of Martin's book:

> Suffering is not the will of God in the sense that God decrees that a certain tragedy shall happen and at a particular time. God has made a world in which the possibility of suffering exists. When that possibility becomes a reality, He normally allows it, not because He wills it so, but because the constitution of the world permits it.
>
> Far from being the deliberate wish of God, the bulk of human suffering is traceable from man's own sin or folly. C. S. Lewis says, "The possibility of pain is inherent in a world where

souls can meet. When souls become wicked there is the possibility to hurt one another. And this, perhaps, accounts for four-fifths of the suffering of men. It is men, not God, who have produced racks and whips, prisons, slavery, guns, bayonets, bombs. It is by human avarice, or human stupidity, not by the churlishness of nature, that we have poverty, and overwork."

Not all of human suffering, of course, can be traced to man's misuse of his free will in this way. Some belongs entirely to the realm of the world as it is, and the laws that govern it.

The world as it is, with its law and order and man's possession of free will—carrying with them, as they do, the risk of suffering—is, we believe, the best possible world for God's loving purpose, the salvation of men. This, however, is a far cry from the belief that suffering is sent by God. If I give my boy a pair of roller skates, I immediately make it possible for him to have a bad bump. That is a very different thing from taking him by the neck and banging his head upon the ground.

The apostle James appears to have taught this distinction as well, separating the *causes of* suffering from the *divine purposes in* suffering. In James 1:12, the apostle states that God uses trials or temptations to test us for approval, and in verse 13 he clearly states that the source of the trial/temptation is not from God.

To me it is a comfort to know that God does not cause my suffering, but that in love He can work out wonderful purposes through my pain. The divine wisdom in the Scriptures reveals to us many of the causes and also many of the divine purposes for suffering.

CAUSES OF SUFFERING

At least four major causes of suffering are revealed in Scripture.

SATAN

In the book of Job, Job felt that when he lost his family, his wealth, and his health, his losses were directly from the hand of God. He was unaware of the realities behind the scene: that Satan was the direct cause of all that he suffered. Much that happens in the world is under the domain of Satan.

THE SIN OF ADAM

According to Romans 5 and 8, the world is under the dominion of sin and judged by God because we—mankind—under the leadership of our first parent, Adam, sinned. We rebelled against the God who had placed us here to rule this planet. We placed ourselves under Satan and in so doing placed the entire planet under Satan.

Romans 8 speaks of the world as "groaning" because it is now under bondage. This fallen world, under Satan's domain, is affected by hurricanes, earthquakes, and other natural catastrophes that plague mankind.

PERSONAL SINS

James explains that what we do that is sinful ultimately brings forth terrible consequences. "But each one is tempted when he is drawn away by his own desires and enticed. Then, when desire has conceived, it gives birth to sin; and sin, when it is full-grown, brings forth death" (James 1:14-15). If we are honest, it is not hard to see the pain and suffering we cause for ourselves through our own sin. Immorality produces disease; anger produces conflicts and ulcers; selfishness produces broken relationships; law-breaking produces civil punishment.

THE SINS OF OTHERS

We live in a fallen world in which other fallen creatures live, and we suffer because of the sins of other people. A drunken driver destroys an innocent family in a wreck. A megalomaniac ruler enslaves his people and forces the world into war. A compassionless society fails to provide for the hurting and the homeless. James also addresses this cause of suffering: "Where do wars and fights come from among you? Do they not come from your desires for pleasure that war in your members? You lust and do not have. You murder and covet and cannot obtain.

You fight and war. Yet you do not have because you do not ask" (James 4:1-2).

DIVINE PURPOSES IN SUFFERING

Although God is not the direct cause of suffering in the life of the believer, we recognize that our God is sovereign, and that He is not limited by the effects of sin in carrying out His purposes for His people. The book of Romans states this truth clearly: "And we know that all things work together for good to those who love God, to those who are the called according to His purpose" (Romans 8:28).

The implication of Romans 8:28 is that whatever Satan might do, God can show mercy and ultimately turn what Satan does into something good for those who love Him. In other words, we can be assured that God is working out wonderful purposes both for our good and for His glory through the suffering that He allows in our lives. Though certainly not exhaustive, following are six specific purposes God may be working out in our lives through our suffering and our pain.

Purpose #1. Suffering in life ultimately will bring glory to God

After Jesus had healed a man who had suffered as a blind man since birth, He stated God's ultimate purpose for the man's suffering: "Neither this man nor his parents sinned, but that the works of God should be revealed in him" (John 9:3). Paul similarly acknowledged this purpose in his life and death: "According to my earnest expectation and hope that in nothing I shall be ashamed, but that with all boldness, as always, so now also Christ will be magnified in my body, whether by life or by death" (Philippians 1:20).

Purpose #2. Suffering can enhance our witness for Christ

In 2 Corinthians Paul asserts that the suffering he has endured in this life will ultimately be used for the spread of the gospel:

We are hard pressed on every side, yet not crushed; we are perplexed, but not in despair; persecuted, but not forsaken; struck down, but not destroyed—always carrying about in the body the dying of the Lord Jesus, that the life of Jesus also may be manifested in our body. For we who live are always delivered to death for Jesus' sake, that the life of Jesus also may be manifested in our mortal flesh. (2 Corinthians 4:8-11)

Paul also emphasized this truth in Philippians 2:12-30.

The vicious killing of Wycliffe Translator missionary Chet Bitterman in South America at the hands of radicals a few years ago has actually resulted in a positive witness for the name of Christ. So has it always been when Christians have been martyred throughout the centuries.

One of the confrontive early church authors, Tertullian, wrote these stirring words in an era of aggressive persecution against Christians:

Give us now what names you please from your instruments of cruelty which you torture us by. Call us Sarmenticians and Semaxians, because you fasten us to trunks of trees and you stick us about with faggots to set us on fire, yet let me tell you that when we are thus begirt and we are dressed about with fire, we are then in our most illustrious apparel. These are our victorious palms and robes of glory. And mounted upon our funeral pile, we look upon ourselves in our triumphal chariot.

And now, oh worshipful judges, go on with your show of justice, and, believe me, you will be juster and juster still in the opinion of the people the oftener you make them sacrifice of Christians. Crucify, torture, condemn, grind us all to powder, if you can; your injustice is an illustrious proof of our innocence. And for the proof of this it is that God permits us to suffer; . . . it is all to no purpose; you do but attract the world, and make it fall the more in love with our religion; the more you mow us down, the thicker we rise. The Christian blood you spill is like the seed you sow. It springs from the earth again and fructifies the more.

Thus has been the history of the church. The church has frequently grown significantly during times of suffering. In Ethiopia prior to the end of World War II, when missionaries were driven out, there was a subsequent expansion of the gospel. In China the gospel has spread rapidly under Communist rule. In Eastern Europe and Russia there are signs that the gospel of Jesus Christ is alive and well, and some observe that the eastern European church is stronger than that which exists in the West. God often uses the suffering of His people to be a mighty witness for Him.

Purpose #3. God uses suffering to develop godly characteristics in us such as patience, endurance, and humility

Both James and Paul wrote of the special place suffering can and does have in our lives in the developing of godly qualities:

> My brethren, count it all joy when you fall into various trials, knowing that the testing of your faith produces patience. (James 1:2-3)

> And lest I should be exalted above measure by the abundance of revelations, a thorn in the flesh was given to me, a messenger of Satan to buffet me, lest I be exalted above measure. (2 Corinthians 12:7)

Purpose #4. God sometimes uses suffering in our lives to illustrate divine truth to others

This purpose was revealed through the life of the prophet Hosea. The prophet's wife left him and became a prostitute and slave. Later, Hosea had to go to the slave market to buy her back. God used this tragic experience to illustrate His great love for the nation of Israel.

Purpose #5. Suffering sometimes is used by God as divine discipline for our sins

When we stop walking with the Lord, He disciplines us as a father does a son to restore us to fellowship with Him. This purpose is captured in Hebrews: "And you have forgotten the exhortation which speaks to you as to sons: 'My son, do not despise the chastening of the Lord, nor be discouraged when you are rebuked by Him; for whom the Lord loves He chastens, and scourges every son whom He receives'" (Hebrews 12:5-6).

Purpose #6. God uses suffering to more fully manifest the sufficiency of His grace in us

In 2 Corinthians Paul says that suffering is an opportunity for God to manifest in powerful fashion that His grace is sufficient to maintain the life of the believer under any and all circumstances. After describing a physical infirmity he had as a thorn in the flesh, Paul wrote:

> Concerning this thing I pleaded with the Lord three times that it might depart from me. And He said to me, "My grace is sufficient for you, for My strength is made perfect in weakness." Therefore most gladly I will rather boast in my infirmities, that the power of Christ may rest upon me. Therefore I take pleasure in infirmities, in reproaches, in needs, in persecutions, in distresses, for Christ's sake. For when I am weak, then I am strong. (2 Corinthians 12:8-10)

EXPERIENCE THE LOVE OF GOD PERSONALLY

Knowing that God is not the ultimate cause of suffering is often encouraging. It also helps us to know and understand that God is busy in His sovereign grace working the things we suffer for good for us. But the greatest strengthening of the suffering saint takes place when he personally experiences God's loving comfort.

At the close of James's teaching on trials, he focuses our attention on the special loving relationship we have with our heavenly Father. "Do not be deceived, my beloved brethren. Every good gift and every perfect gift is from above, and comes down from the Father of lights, with whom there is no variation or shadow of turning" (James 1:16-17).

James is telling us that God loves us. We are greatly helped in the face of suffering by having an eternal perspective and by gaining a wise perspective that distinguishes between the causes and purposes of suffering. But ultimately the only real comfort comes when we run to our father and experience his infinite love.

I remember well the warmth of Jesus' loving touch as I knelt alone and prayed right after my earthly father died. Such comfort often comes directly to our souls from God, and it also may come through loving Christian friends, but either way, experiencing God's love is the best way to find strength to persevere through the hard times.

A Final Thought

James encourages us to persevere under suffering, recognizing that God loves us and is the source of the good things He is doing in our lives. Don't run from your heavenly Father. Run *to* Him.

15

The Crown of Joy
(Exultation) and Evangelism

The third wreath-crown is the *crown of rejoicing,* or *exultation.* It is referred to in two different passages by Paul:

> For what is our hope, or joy, or crown of rejoicing? Is it not even you in the presence of our Lord Jesus Christ at His coming? For you are our glory and joy. (1 Thessalonians 2:19-20)

> Therefore, my beloved and longed-for brethren, my joy and crown, so stand fast in the Lord, beloved. (Philippians 4:1)

JOYFUL EXULTATION

This crown is often called the "crown of joy" because of the reference to joy (Greek *chara*) in close connection with the reference to the crown. Paul identifies this crown with the people he has led to the Lord, and at the same time he calls these same people his joy in the presence of Christ. So the term *crown of joy* is certainly an appropriate one. But to be more precise, Paul actually gives the name of this crown as the "crown of rejoicing," or "crown of exultation." The word translated "rejoicing" in 1 Thessalonians 2 is *kauchesis,* which may be translated in various related ways: "boasting," "whereof I may glory," "rejoicing," "glorying," "proud confidence," "have great pride," and "exultation." All of those translations are attempts to capture the basic meaning and the connotations of the word. Perhaps the best way to picture the meaning is to compare it to the emotions the nation experienced at the close of the ground war in the Persian Gulf War. The president, the troops, and the nation as a whole experienced an overwhelming sense of pride and euphoria. The term *kauchesis* would be a good word to describe the deep pride, joy, and exultation that we all experienced.

So it will be that, when we stand in the presence of Jesus at His royal coming, our hearts will overflow with pride, joy, and exultation because of those who stand with us at that time —those we have had a share in bringing to the Savior.

What a thrill! For all eternity we will have "walking wreath-crowns" living and enjoying with us the glorious presence and unspeakable delights of life in the kingdom of the Prince of Peace.

It is one of the great blessings in life to have a foretaste of that wonderful day. A middle aged couple—leaders in their church and in the Christian community—met me for dinner, thanking me for sharing the gospel with them fifteen years earlier. What a wonderful experience! Recently a young man, who is a CPA for the state of Colorado and who attends my businessmen's Bible study, made an appointment with me. The reason: He wanted to tell me that he had recently accepted Christ at the Bible study and had joined a Bible-teaching, evangelical church, where he was already being trained through Evangelism Explosion. Wow! Multiply this experience by everyone you have had a part in leading to Christ and then envision such an experience in heaven in the presence of Jesus. That will be a time of incomparable exultation. And better still it will be a reward that has feet and is present in the new heavens and new earth forever.

Winning the Crowns of Joy

As we win people to Christ, we are in fact winning the very ones that will be our crowns of joyful exultation in the presence of Jesus in heaven at the *bema*.

The Scriptures make clear that this crown can be won by any believer. In fact the implication of the great commission given to the apostles is that all of us who know Jesus, because we have been given the presence of the Holy Spirit, have been ordained to be witnesses for Christ: "But you shall receive power when the Holy Spirit has come upon you; and you shall be witnesses to Me in Jerusalem, and in all Judea and Samaria, and to the end of the earth" (Acts 1:8).

Some Christians assume that the work of telling the good news about Jesus to people that don't know Him is assigned either to the person who is a gifted evangelist or to the church's staff ministers. On the contrary, Paul specifically taught that the evangelists and the pastors and teachers were not given to the church to be the only ones who do the work of the ministry. Rather, those gifted persons (along with the gifts of apostle and prophet, which were given to lay the foundation of the church —see Ephesians 2:20) were given primarily to equip (train) the individual believer (saint) so that he or she could do the work of ministry that builds the church. Referring to Christ's gracious provision of spiritual gifts to the church when He ascended into heaven, Paul wrote, "And He Himself gave some to be apostles, some prophets, some evangelists, and some pastors and teachers, for the equipping of the saints for the work of ministry, for the edifying of the body of Christ" (Ephesians 4:11-12). So not only can any Christian win this special prize, but Christ expects all of us to at least have a share in these crowns.

We can share in the crown of joyful exultation in at least three different ways: (1) by personally sharing the gospel with someone in the power of the Holy Spirit, trusting the results to God; (2) by contributing to the winning of someone to Christ through such activities as inviting a friend to church or to an evangelistic meeting, or by assisting in the evangelistic activities of others in some way; and (3) by supporting the ministry of evangelists and missionaries (remember that Jesus promised a share in the reward given to a prophet or a righteous man that we "receive," or make provision for—Matthew 10:40-41).

THE MESSAGE

In order to bring people to Christ we need to make sure that our message is clear. In the Bible that message is called the "gospel," which is a translation of the Greek word *euangelion,* which literally means "good news." The communication of the gospel is called "evangelism," a translation of a similar Greek word, *euangelizo,* which literally means "to carry the message of the good news to others."

THE DOCTRINAL BASIS FOR THE GOSPEL

More specifically, the gospel is the message of good news that a person needs to hear and understand and to which he can respond and thus experience God's forgiveness, new life, and the blessings of God's eternal new heavens and new earth. Because all of us are sinners, God's justice demands that all of us be judged with eternal death in hell (Romans 3:23; 6:23). The good news is that God's justice has been satisfied by the sacrificial death of His infinitely valuable, sinless, perfectly righteous son, the Lord Jesus Christ (Romans 5:8; 2 Corinthians 5:21). Furthermore, Jesus was raised from the dead, and all who are joined to Him share in His resurrection life (Ephesians 4:2-6).

What then must a person do to receive God's forgiveness and the gift of eternal life that begins in this life? Using the term *saved* to refer to these divine provisions, Luke records Paul's answer to this question, when it was posed by his jailer in Philippi: "And he brought them out and said, 'Sirs, what must I do to be saved?' So they said, 'Believe on the Lord Jesus Christ, and you will be saved, you and your household'" (Acts 16:30-31).

That is the same answer the Scriptures repeatedly give, using many synonyms, such as "trust," "repent" (which basically means "change your mind about your need for Christ and His provision for you"), "receive," "accept," and "have faith." (See such passages as John 3 and 4; Romans 4 and 11; and Ephesians 2.) Because we can do nothing to get ourselves out of the predicament of our sin and its consequences, every part of our salvation depends entirely on God's grace and the provision for forgiveness and life in Jesus.

As a child I was confused concerning the gospel and was left with no assurance of my relationship with God. I had got the impression that in some way my salvation depended on me. One day I picked up a tract that said there were four things I needed to do in order to be saved. Before those thoughts crystallized in my mind, I found another tract that said there were seven things I needed to do to be saved. I was confused and plagued with doubt. Then one day I read a booklet by George Cutting titled *Safety, Certainty, and Enjoyment.* Cutting made clear that there was nothing that I could do to participate in my salvation. Jesus did it all. All I needed to do was to respond by accepting the free gift of forgiveness and life by trusting in Jesus. In his epistles Paul made clear that salvation is a free gift from God provided entirely by His grace (His love in action), and that adding something else to our faith eliminates grace:

> For by grace you have been saved through faith, and that not of yourselves; it is the gift of God, not of works, lest anyone should boast. (Ephesians 2:8-9)

> For what does the Scripture say? "Abraham believed God, and it was accounted to him for righteousness." Now to him who works, the wages are not counted as grace but as debt. But to him who does not work, but believes on Him who justifies the ungodly, his faith is accounted for righteousness. (Romans 4:3-5)

> And if by grace, then it is no longer of works; otherwise grace is no longer grace. But if it is works, it is no longer grace; otherwise work is no longer work. (Romans 11:6)

In other words, receiving God's wonderful gift of forgiveness and life depends entirely on Him and our receiving His gift of life by faith in His son. Our good works, our promises, our tears, our church membership, our religious activities, our baptism, even our attempt to build up a faith strong enough to produce good works—all of those can add absolutely nothing to the completed work of Christ. In fact, to depend on any of those is to replace Christ's work and God's grace with our own efforts, leaving us still hopelessly without God's gracious provisions.

THE GOSPEL

Paul makes clear what the gospel is. In 1 Corinthians he declares that the gospel is not connected to a work of man, such as baptism, and that the gospel is the message about Jesus and what He did for us. Read carefully Paul's transparent statements:

> For Christ did not send me to baptize, but to preach the gospel, not with wisdom of words, lest the cross of Christ should be made of no effect. For the message of the cross is foolishness to those who are perishing, but to us who are being saved it is the power of God. (1 Corinthians 1:17-18)

> Moreover, brethren, I declare to you the gospel which I preached to you, which also you received and in which you stand, by which also you are saved, if you hold fast that word which I preached to you—unless you believed in vain. For I delivered to you first of all that which I also received: that Christ died for our sins according to the Scriptures, and that He was buried, and that He rose again the third day according to the Scriptures, and that He was seen. (1 Corinthians 15:1-5*a*)

The gospel is the message that Jesus did it all. He died for our sins, and He was raised bodily from the grave. Salvation all depends on Him.

A GOSPEL PRESENTATION

In presenting this wonderful message we normally need to give our listeners some other truths along with it, so that the true significance of the gospel can be understood. Following is a simple summary of those truths: (1) There is a personal, living God who is both perfectly just and infinitely loving. (2) All of us, and each of us in particular, have sinned and are sinners deserving God's judgment and separation from Him forever in hell. (3) The good news (gospel) is that Jesus is the fulfillment of the scriptural promise of the coming Messiah who would pay the penalty for our sins by dying on the cross, and He, the resurrected Lord, can give us life. (4) The only necessary response to Jesus and His completed, saving work is to trust in Him.

REFERENCE TO THE LORDSHIP OF CHRIST IN A GOSPEL PRESENTATION

Responding to the widespread moral and spiritual compromise in Christendom, many today seek to emphasize the importance of the lordship of Christ in the presentation of the gospel, arguing that true saving faith is a persevering faith that has submitted to the lordship of Christ. Others take a different position, arguing that by including the lordship of Christ in the presentation of the gospel we leave the impression that our salvation is dependent not on Christ alone but on our willingness to obey Him and on our ability to muster up a strong enough faith from within ourselves that will produce a holy life, a faith strong enough to persevere through any trial that lies ahead.

I am forced to agree that the lordship of Christ should not be included in the presentation of the gospel. The Scriptures emphasize that salvation is by grace through faith and that man is totally helpless to do anything whatsoever to earn his salvation. The production of holiness and perseverance in the life of a Christian is a work of God that begins at rebirth after he trusts Christ. It is therefore the product of regeneration, not the expression of some kind of faith that is worked up in the heart of a lost man before he gets saved.

However, I might add that a good gospel presentation does in fact include not only an emphasis on simple trust but also a presentation of Jesus as both Lord and Savior. On the one hand, we need to make certain our hearers in no way are left with the impression that their salvation depends on them, their feelings, their deeds, or even how much faith they can build up. Rather it depends entirely on Christ, and it is appropriated by the simplest of trust in Him. On the other hand, a clear gospel message must clearly state who Jesus is and that He is Lord, with all that that signifies: He is God, the Son, the second Person of the Trinity; He is Lord by resurrection from the dead, the conqueror of sin and death; He is the anointed (Messiah) king with all authority given to Him in heaven and on earth. Anyone who accepts His free gift of salvation automatically becomes not only a member of His family but also Christ's purchased possession under His authority and His loving discipline.

We might visualize our faith in Christ this way. A man has the ball and chain of sin attached to his ankles and is being pulled steadily toward destruction. He realizes his plight; he turns around (repents) and reaches out to the King of kings, the Lord Jesus Christ, to deliver him. The man makes no promises, for he has no ability of his own to make any. He changes nothing of any real importance in his life, for he cannot. He reaches out to Jesus and to Jesus alone for deliverance (salvation) from sin and hell and for new life—life eternal. He accepts Christ for who He is—Lord and Messiah-King, for to do anything else would be to place his hope in a false Jesus (see 2 Corinthians 11:4); and he rests his entire hope for heaven in the Lord Jesus, and in Him alone.

To acknowledge that Jesus is Lord in a helpless faith-reach of a lost man is a far cry, however, from trying to build up enough faith to be able to commit to Jesus in advance that he will serve Him as Lord in purity and perseverance. So I would conclude that a gospel presentation that is in keeping with the truth of Scripture is one that presents Jesus as Lord and Christ but carefully avoids confusing the hearer with any requirement that he must be able to believe deeply enough to commit to obediently follow Jesus no matter what temptation or trial he might face.

THE MAN

The Bible clarifies what the gospel message is and also describes an effective evangelist, a sharer of the good news. In 1 Thessalonians 2, in the verses preceding his reference to the crown of joyful exultation, Paul provides a description of the characteristics of the kind of gospel communication he had exhibited at Thessalonica.

He says that his coming to Thessalonica to preach the gospel had certain observable characteristics: (1) not in vain (v. 1) —that is, not void of divine power; with a witness that was in the power of the Holy Spirit; (2) with boldness even in the face of opposition (v. 2); (3) not based on the deceit of false doctrine (v. 3); (4) without any immorality on his part as an evangelist (v. 3); (5) honest and aboveboard (v. 3); (6) with a desire to be approved by God, not to please men (v. 4); (7) without flattering speech (v. 5); (8) not out of greed (v. 5); (9) free from self-glorification (v. 6); (10) with gentleness (v. 7); (11) with love for them (v. 8); and (12) not allowing his financial needs to become a barrier to his being able to minister to them (v. 9).

Furthermore, in 1 Thessalonians 2:10-12, Paul describes his follow-up ministry to them in the two or three weeks he had with them before having to leave for his missionary thrust into southern Greece. He began the process of developing them into committed disciples of Christ through four specific ministries to them: (1) he was an example to them in behavior—He was devout (demonstrated a close personal walk with God), he was just, or righteous (living consistently with high ethical standards), and he was blameless (avoiding even those things that might appear to be wrong); (2) he exhorted them in an encouraging way to live a similar kind of life as disciples of Christ; (3) he comforted them during the difficult times; and (4) he charged them as a father does his children to walk worthy of God and His kingdom.

THE METHODS

Perhaps you really want to go for the crown of joyful exultation by being a part of winning others to Christ, but you feel intimidated by those who seem to know more Bible doctrine, or by those who find it easy to talk to other people—even strangers—about almost anything. Or perhaps you have been scared away by high-pressure approaches. Let me suggest a few ideas that might open exciting and unexpected doors for you. Besides the obvious church and para-church strategies, such as home visitation and evangelistic meetings, pray about using one or more of the following:

1. Pass out tracts or leave them on the table at a restaurant. Be sure that the tract is attractive and clearly presents the gospel. Also always give a generous tip (15 percent or more) when you leave a tract. I personally like this method because I was saved through reading a tract.

2. Invite someone who is new in the church to your home for dinner. The expression of love through hospitality can be one of the most powerful evangelistic tools.

3. Invite a friend to church or to a special evangelistic gathering.

4. Start a Bible study geared for the non-Christian—at home or at your school, office, or shop.

5. At work over lunch or on break read interesting Christian books that provoke interest in spiritual things, such as good books on personal needs and pains or on prophecy.

6. Teach a Sunday school class and once each year have the students answer a list of questions that indicate whether or not they have trusted Christ personally. Then set up an appointment after Sunday school or after school or work to have a Coke or coffee and share the gospel with them.

7. Spend time with a ministry that reaches out to those in need, perhaps a food service or tutoring ministry in the inner city.

8. Participate in a church recreation program for young people geared especially to minister to the single-parent child.

9. Have a coffee in your home for neighbors and invite in a special speaker who will share about his or her faith.

10. Develop a welcome ministry of coffee and cake for every new resident in a nearby apartment complex.

Those are but a few to get you going. The most effective evangelistic outreach takes place in a context where you can live and express the love of Christ.

MAKE THE *BEMA* A TIME OF EXULTATION

No matter what loss or even possible shame that may appear at the *bema,* we can make sure that it will be a time of unspeakable, joyous exultation if we begin now to allow the Spirit of God to use us to win men and women, and boys and girls to faith in the Savior. Ray Boltz captures a little of the thrill and wonder of the recognition of the crowns of joy on that day in his moving Christian ballad "Thank You":

Thank You

Words and music by Ray Boltz

I dreamed I went to heaven; you were there
    with me.
We walked upon the streets of gold beside the
    crystal sea.
We heard the angels singing, then someone
    called your name.
You turned and saw the young man; he was
    smiling as he came.

And he said, "Friend you may not know me
    now."
Then he said, "But wait! You used to teach my
    Sunday School when I was only eight.
And ev'ry week you would say a prayer before
    the class would start.
And one day when you said that prayer, I
    asked Jesus in my heart."

(Chorus)
"Thank you for giving to the Lord;
I am a life that was changed.
Thank you for giving to the Lord;
I am so glad you gave!"

Then another man stood before you. He said,
    "Remember the time
A missionary came to your church; his pic-
    tures made you cry?
You didn't have much money, but you gave it
    anyway.
Jesus took the gift you gave; that's why I'm
    here today."

(Chorus)

One by one they came, far as the eye could
    see,
Each life somehow touched by your
    generosity.
Little things that you had done, sacrifices
    made,
Unnoticed on the earth, in heaven now
    proclaimed.

I know up in heaven you're not supposed to
    cry,
But I am almost sure there were tears in your
    eyes.
As Jesus took your hand, you stood before the
    Lord;
He said, "My child, look around you, for great
    is your reward!"

(Chorus)

16

The Crown of Glory and Christlike Leaders

The last wreath-crown we will study is the *crown of glory*. This crown is referred to in the apostle Peter's first epistle. In the last chapter of the book he addresses the leaders of the church:

> The elders who are among you I exhort, I who am a fellow elder and a witness of the sufferings of Christ, and also a partaker of the glory that will be revealed: shepherd the flock of God which is among you, serving as overseers, not by constraint but willingly, not for dishonest gain but eagerly; nor as being lords over those entrusted to you, but being examples to the flock; and when the Chief Shepherd appears, you will receive the crown of glory that does not fade away. (1 Peter 5:1-4)

Over the years in the ministry I have seen the terrific pressure and high expectations laid upon the leaders of churches. Many elders and pastors throw in the towel or fail as spiritual leaders, while others hang in there and attempt to imitate the Chief Shepherd as well as they can—often being misunderstood and criticized unjustly. So it is not surprising to me that the Lord reserves a special crown for these noble leaders of the flock of God.

WHAT IS AN ELDER?

Peter calls himself and the leaders of the church "elders." The term he employs is the Greek term *presbuteros,* which literally means "an old man." It was the term used by the Jews to refer to members of the Jewish Council, or Sanhedrin, and it also was used of the officials who were in charge of the Jewish synagogue. A Latin equivalent was the word *senator.* It was used in the New Testament for the leaders of the local churches that were appointed by the apostles. Later the term was modified by the Roman Church into the term *priest.* All of the usages point to the common meaning of organizational leadership.

To better understand what Peter is driving at, we need to survey how the church of Peter's day understood the title *elder.* In the New Testament the office of *presbuteros* is equated to the office of *episcopos.* In Titus 1:5 the leaders of the church are called "elders" (*presbuteroi*), and two verses later one of those same leaders is called a "bishop" (*episcopos,* a term also translated in some English translations by the word "overseer"). It is instructive to note that there is no specific office of pastor mentioned in the New Testament. Rather the function of pastoring or shepherding is to be carried on by the elder-bishops (1 Peter 5:2; Acts 20:28).

From this biblical evidence and the influence of history, Christian churches have evolved three different forms of church government. One is the presbyterian form of government, characterized by the leadership of a group of men that are called elders. The second is the congregational form of government, characterized by its entrusting the leadership of the church to a pastor. The third is the hierarchal form, characterized by its placing authority in the hands of a priest who serves under a hierarchy of bishops. Notice that all three forms employ one of the biblical terms for leadership.

Although I have a preference as to which form of church government most closely follows the pattern of the first-century church, I am sure the Lord is far less concerned about the precise form of government than He is about the quality and character of the leadership in place. Thus it is likely that the crown of glory is reserved for faithful leaders in all churches who carry out their responsibilities in accordance with Peter's clear guidelines

PETER THE ELDER

Peter identified himself as one of the leaders in the church and articulated the experiences that qualified him to be able to charge all other elders. He had been an eyewitness of the sufferings of Christ, watching Jesus being arrested, falsely charged, beaten, and sentenced to death on the cross. But he had also been a partaker of the glory that will be revealed in the coming kingdom. He, along with James and John, had been with Jesus on the mountain in Palestine when Jesus was transfigured before them, and he had seen and heard Jesus conversing with the resuscitated Moses and Elijah about his impending "exodus," or departure (Luke 9:27-36). That experience overshadowed Peter's entire ministry, for he referred to it again in his second epistle:

> For we did not follow cunningly devised fables when we made know to you the power and coming of our Lord Jesus Christ, but were eyewitnesses of His majesty. For He received from God the Father honor and glory when such a voice came to Him from the Excellent Glory: "This is My beloved Son, in whom I am well pleased." And we heard this voice which came from heaven when we were with him on the holy mountain. (2 Peter 1:16-18)

So in an attempt to emphasize the importance of what he is about to say, Peter introduced his exhortation with a reminder of the special relationship he had had with the Chief Shepherd, Jesus.

RESPONSIBILITIES OF THE ELDERS

Peter summarized the responsibilities of the church leaders (elders) in two broad statements. First, church leaders were to shepherd the flock of God. The flock, he reminded them, is in fact not theirs, but God's. In that flock were many sheep and helpless lambs with very special needs.

The elders had a number of specific responsibilities as shepherds, as Paul and James observed in other passages of Scripture: (1) In Acts 20:28-31 Paul told the Ephesian elders that as leaders they were to *guard the flock* from those who would harm them spiritually, false teachers in particular. (2) In Titus 1:9 Paul asserted that leaders are to *feed the flock* with teaching and exhortation. (3) In James 5:14 James reminded the leaders of their responsibility to *pray for the sick.*

The elders also had specific responsibilities as overseers of the flock, specifically to carry out tasks of *administration, leadership,* and *rule.* Of course this ruling was strictly qualified in 1 Peter 5, but the leaders were indeed to lead. That role of the church leaders is what the writer of the epistle to the Hebrews had in mind when he wrote, "Remember those who rule over you, who have spoken the word of God to you, whose faith follow, considering the outcome of their conduct" (Hebrews 13:7).

GUIDELINES FOR GODLY ELDERS

After giving the general responsibilities of church leaders (elders), Peter gave strict guidelines for their behavior, by which they would be evaluated at the *bema* of Christ when the special crowns for faithful leadership were dispensed.

First, church leaders should accept leadership responsibilities out of love and the desire to please the Chief Shepherd, that is, their service should not be "by constraint but willingly" (1 Peter 2:2*a*).

Second, church leaders should not take their positions in order to further their own personal standing or to obtain wealth dishonestly. Rather, they should do it "eagerly" as a means of serving Christ and His church (1 Peter 2:2*b*).

Third, church leaders were to lead by "example," not "lording it over the flock" (1 Peter 2:3). The implication of the context is that the model for shepherding is the Chief Shepherd. As church leaders followed Jesus as disciples, they would become true examples for the flock to follow.

The church of Jesus Christ today is blessed with many leaders who fully carry out their God-given responsibilities, faithfully attempting to function in accordance with clear guidelines. But there are also leaders who compromise the clear teachings of Christ and live lives that are far from exemplary. When the Chief Shepherd appears, Peter declared, He will separate the faithful from the unfaithful church leaders, and for the faithful, the crown of glory.

Some years ago I read a stirring challenge to church leaders by A. W. Tozer. George Verwer, leader of Operation Mobilization, says that he has written Tozer's challenge in the front of one of his Bibles. Here is that challenge.

> The Church at this moment needs men who feel themselves expendable in the warfare of the soul. Such men will be free from the compulsions that control weaker men, the lust of the eyes, the lust of the flesh, and pride of life. They will not be forced to do things by the squeeze of circumstances. Their only compulsion will come from within and from above. This kind of freedom is necessary if we are going to have prophets in our pulpits again instead of mascots. These free men will serve God and men from motives too high to be understood by the rank and file who today shuffle in and out of the sanctuary. They will make no decision out of fear, they will take no course out of a desire to please, accept no service for financial consideration. They will perform no religious act out of mere custom. Nor will they allow themselves to be influenced by the love of publicity, or by the desire for reputation.[1]

Note

1. George Verwer, *Come! Live! Die!* (Wheaton: Tyndale House, 1972), pp. 41-42.

Conclusion

The doctrine of the *bema* of Christ and eternal rewards is one the church needs to hear. There are eternal repercussions in all that the believer thinks, says, and does, and it is only fair that Christians be made aware of those repercussions before it is too late for them to make a change in the way they live. The *bema* can significantly affect our lives. The *bema* and eternal rewards are truths of comfort as well. They can be of great encouragement when we face pressure and criticism from others or endure periods of suffering and persecution.

When we enter into that eternal heavenly fellowship with our Lord and are able to bring praise and worship to Him through the rewards we have received from Him, how grateful we will be that we took heed to the biblical teachings concerning the *bema* and rewards.

In 1978, the *Houston Post* carried the account of a boy named Timmy, who—though he was severely hampered by cerebral palsy—announced to his mother one day that he was going to run in a local mini-marathon. She tried to discourage him, but he was not dissuaded. On the day of the race, though he could barely get himself around the block in good order, Timmy was at the starting line when the race began. As the other racers took off at full stride, he began to move forward slowly, favoring his good left leg and nursing along his unsynchronized right leg as best he could.

Another man won the mini-marathon in 32 minutes and 23 seconds. Timmy crossed the line in 2 hours and 6 minutes—dead last. But, as the headline of the article so accurately recorded, that day "The Real Winner Came in Last."

The life that wins in the race toward the goal line found in the presence of Jesus is the one that finishes. It is not necessarily the life that everyone notices, the life that receives all the glory here on earth, the life that looks good to everyone else. It is the life that is continually aware of and motivated by past blessings and future rewards from God.

If we are truly aware of the greatness of the salvation we have in Christ we will *commit our bodies* as living sacrifices to Him (Romans 12:1,2), we will be *constrained to serve* Him (2 Corinthians 5:14), we will *exhibit character* worthy of our calling (Ephesians 4-5), and we will *display Christian community* with unselfish love (1 John 4).

Similarly, if we are truly aware of seriousness and the reality of the coming judgment seat of Christ, we will keep our *priorities* straight (Luke 21), keep our lives *pure* (1 John 3:3), keep claiming the *promises* of God (Hebrews 4), and keep *persevering* in our faith walk (Hebrews 11; 12).

As I was completing the writing of this book, I had dinner with two elderly Christian sisters, Elsie and Helen, who had recently retired from the school where I serve as president. We had a delightful conversation, spending much of our time discussing the judgment seat of Christ and the perspective each of us had on the doctrine.

Later in the conversation, I asked about their future plans. Elsie shared with me their vision to assist an Hispanic alumnus of our school in planting an Hispanic church in a nearby city. Their involvement had brought them to the conclusion that the Lord would have them sell the home they had lived in for many years and move to the new city. I could tell that selling their home and moving was going to be quite hard for them, but Elsie, quite matter-of-factly, remarked that a house is a material thing that soon will pass away but ministry in the lives of people will last. So she and her sister had been busily cleaning and packing, preparing to move. The eyes of Elsie and Helen were on the goal at the *bema,* as they had been for many years before.

May this study be an encouragement to you as well to run to completion the race that is before you, looking unto Jesus, and making your life count for eternity!

Selected Bibliography

Billheimer, Paul. *Destined for the Throne*. Fort Washington, Pa.: Christian Literature Crusade, 1975.

Chitwood, Arlen L. *Judgment Seat of Christ*. Norman, Okla.: The Lamp Broadcast, 1986.

_____. *Salvation of the Soul*. Norman, Okla.: The Lamp Broadcast, 1986.

Hodges, Zane. *Grace in Eclipse*. Dallas: Redencion Viva, 1985.

Hoyt, Herman. *The End Times*. Chicago: Moody, 1969.

Hoyt, Samuel. "The Judgment Seat of Christ and Unconfessed Sins." *Bibliotheca Sacra*. Dallas: Dallas Theological Seminary, 1980.

Lang, G. H. *Firstborn Sons: Their Rights and Their Risks*. Miami Springs, Fla.: Conley and Schoettle, 1984.

Pache, René. *The Future Life*. Chicago: Moody 1963.

Panton, D. M. *The Judgment Seat of Christ*. Miami Springs, Fla.: Conley and Schoettle, 1983.

Pentecost, J. Dwight. *Things to Come*. Finley, Ohio: Dunham, 1958.

Walvoord, John F. *The Prophecy Knowledge Handbook*. Dallas: Dallas Seminary Press, 1990.

_____. *The Millennial Kingdom*. Findlay, Ohio: Dunham, 1959.

Winter, David. *Hereafter*. Wheaton, Ill.: Harold Shaw and The Christian Book Promotion Trust, 1973.

Wood, Leon. *The Bible and Future Events*. Grand Rapids: Zondervan, 1973.

Index of Subjects

Abiding in Christ. *See* Preparation for the *bema*
After-death experience, 39-52
Angels, 60, 85

Bema (judgment seat), 47-48, 59, 61, 63, 70. *See also* Elders; Negative judgment at the *bema;* Preparation for the *bema;* Rewards
and abiding in Christ, 36
described, 17-18, 31
imminence of, 70-76
impact on life, 18-23
and justification, 27-30, 115
meaning of the term, 32-33
mentality, 74-76
and motives, 20-23, 51, 91-95, 110-17
place of, 50, 67
and prophecy, 63-69
process, 35-36

and salvation, 19, 27-32, 36, 100-101, 115
timing of, 50, 67-68
and works, 24-25, 36-37
Body, glorified. *See* Resurrection bodies

Cherubs, 85
Christ. *See also* Judgment; Second coming of Christ
judge, 25, 34-35
throne of, 88
Condemnation, freedom from, 29, 34
Confession of sin. *See* Preparation for the *bema*
Cross, judgment at. *See* Judgment
Crowns. *See Diadem;* Rewards

Death, 40-43. *See also* Resurrection
intermediate body, 44-45

175

out-of-body experiences,
42-43
permanent, 41-43
reversible, 41-43
second, 52 n. 2, 88, 114
spiritual, 52 n. 2
Deeds, 91
Diadem, 124-26
Discipleship. *See* Ministry

Elders, 165-69
Encouragement, 23, 170
Enemies, love of. *See* Preparation for the *bema*
Eternal state, 64
Evangelism. *See* Ministry

Faith, persevering. *See* Preparation for the *bema*

Glorified bodies. *See* Resurrection
Gospel
content, 155-59
presentation of, 157-62
Great white throne judgment, 25-27, 31, 55
Guidance, divine, 131-39

Heaven, 48, 54-62
Hell, 34, 115
Hindrances to rewards, 112
Holy Spirit, role of. *See* Preparation for the *Bema*

Imminence of the *bema*. *See* Bema
Inheritance. *See* Rewards

Intermediate body. *See* Death

Joy, wreath-crown of. *See* Rewards
Judging angels, 85
Judging others, 85. *See also* Negative judgment at the *bema*
Judgment. *See also Bema;* Negative judgment at the *bema;* Preparation for the *bema*
of believers at the *bema,* 29-30, 31-37, 91-103
of believers at the cross, 27-29
of others, 102
of unbelievers, 25-26, 88
Judgment seat. *See Bema*
Justification. *See Bema*

Kingdom of God, 83
Kingdom of heaven, 106

Lake of fire, 26-27, 52 n. 2,
Lamb's Book of Life, 26-27
Leadership in the church. *See* Elders; Preparation for the *bema*
Length of spiritual life. *See* Preparation for the *bema*
Lordship salvation, 159
Loss of rewards. *See* Negative judgment at the *bema*
Love
for Christ's appearing, 67, 127-28, 132